The Ultimate Kalorik Maxx Air Fryer Oven Cookbook

Easy Kalorik Air Fryer Oven Recipes for Beginners and Advanced Users

By William S. Ferebee

CONTENT

Introduction

Cooking is my passion, and I love to experiment with new recipes. Also, I am open to using new cooking appliances, learning the different features, and making cooking a wonderful experience. My new cookbook features 110 recipes, and I have tailored all the recipes to cook with Kalorik 26 QT Maxx Air Fryer Oven. I have applied a conscious effort in the cookbook to make the cooking a fun-filled experience and written in a simple format targeting beginners.

The recipes cover both veg and non-veg dishes. Besides, the recipes explore through breakfast, lunch, snacks, dinner, etc. You will find the dishes extremely sumptuous and healthy. My sole aim in using the Kalorik Maxx air fryer is to minimize oil consumption while cooking Excessive intake of oil is a reason for developing health-related issues, such as obese and cardiac problems. Special care has applied while selecting ingredients to make sure that the ingredients are available even in the small groceries.

Let me introduce some of the Kalorik 26 QT Digital Maxx Air Fryer Oven's wonderful features and utilities.

Ever since the introduction of Air Fryers in the market, it has undergone many innovations, and new generation air fryers come with lots of features. The air fryers are easy to use, and that is why many people continue to use this cooking appliance, and the new features allow the user to make different dishes with less maneuver.

A Quick Look at the Features & Specs

- Multifunctional
- 30% faster cooking
- No or low oil consumption
- Reduce fat up to 75%
- 21 presets for cooking
- LED screen
- Sears and caramelization at 500°F
- No heat radiation on the body
- Double door made of French glass with handle

- Dehydration features
- Stainless steel body
- Dishwasher safe
- Weight 17.2lb
- Capacity 26 Qtrs.
- Nine accessories
- Voltage 120V
- Wattage 1700W
- Dimension 14" H x 12.4" W x 12.4" D
- 1-year warranty

ETL Certified

Kalorik 26 QT Maxx Air Fryer Oven is the ultimate solution for all your cooking requirements, and it can use as an air fryer and an oven. It is an all in one cooking appliance that makes cooking a lot easier. Kalorik is a trustworthy brand and has been in the market for the last 9 decades. They indeed created a legacy by providing excellent service for years. For generations, Kalorik air fryers have been one of the most favorites of food lovers and have become an essential part of modern kitchens.

Belgium based ETL certified kitchen appliance brand has been our family choice for three generations. The manufacturer has been maintaining high-quality engineering and innovations to match the market trend and demand. The appliance is selling with a one-year warranty, which is an assurance of quality and performance.

It Has Changed My Cooking Preferences.

The ease of cooking with Kalorik Maxx Air Fryer has changed my culinary preferences. The first and foremost is making oil-less food. It is a wonderful accomplishment from a health point of view. I had never thought, cooking with Kalorik Maxx will add that much value to a healthy life.

Recipe for the Beginners

The recipes I have included in the cookbook are suitable for beginners as well as for experienced ones. So, it doesn't matter if you are new to cooking and have no previous experiences. The air fryer with combo features is perfect to meet my cooking requirement, and I hope readers will find the appliance beneficial for various types of cooking. All the recipes you can see in the cookbook are easy to prepare, and you can make delicious and healthy food within a short period without much effort.

The cookbook has 110 recipes, which I have tried and fine-tuned to confirm its taste and crispness. I must say that I have gained a lot of appreciation from my dear ones for the foods served by this appliance.

Whether it is breakfast, lunch, dinner, or any meal, you can prepare it with an air fryer oven. The recipe varieties range from veggies, meat, seafood, snacks, poultry, vegan foods, rotisseries, gourmet, to breakfast recipes, etc. You can sear at 500°F, grill, broil, toast, roast, fry, and bake the dishes the way you want. Its 21 preset options let you select the cooking for your preferred choice of food at your fingertips. Show your passion for cooking with the Kalorik Maxx air fryer oven cookbook for beginners.

Informative LED Screen

The air fryer comes with a relatively clean and clutter-free instruction manual, which I found very helpful to operate the air fryer efficiently. Apart from that, the LED display positioned on the top portion of the oven, facing the user, makes it quite convenient to operate without much confusion. You can preset all cooking options by turning the dial knob as per your choice, and the air fryer will take care of the cooking the way you want.

Follow the Cooking Instructions

Like I mentioned before, it doesn't matter if you are a newbie in cooking. You need to follow the recipe instructions, which are well written and can execute effortlessly by following the cooking direction.

Time Saver

Is cooking a difficult task, and you have no time for cooking? Once you start using Kalorik, it won't be an issue at all. I found the air fryer oven was a savior on many occasions where I had to prepare meals in a rush. Even during some friends' surprise visits, it helped me to fill their stomach with yummy foods.

I have tried a few popular kitchen appliances in the past, but while comparing those with Kalorik, I choose Kalorik Maxx over the rest. Cooking has become an easy and time-saving assignment for me since I began using this air fryer. You can also prepare tasty and healthy foods using the Kalorik Maxx Air Fryer Oven.

Accessories

The air fryer oven comes with 9 cooking accessories: air frying basket, air rack, rack handle, rotisserie handle, rotisserie spit & forks, 2-in-1 dehydrator, and steak tray, crumb tray, bacon tray, and baking pan. The 2-in-1 dehydrator is extremely useful for dehydrating fruits and vegetables in no time. The process lets you not depend on a microwave oven anymore, and you don't have to hunt for microwave-safe cookware now and then.

Benefits of 10 Appliances in One Machine

The air fryer can do 10 different appliance functions without altering or using attachments. The appliance can function like a broiler, toaster, countertop oven, roaster, dehydrator, rotisserie, pizza oven, slow cooker, and grill. I am content with its multipurpose functions, and that is why I want to introduce the Kalorik Maxx Air fryer Oven to all my readers.

My Cooking Experience with Kalorik

It is one of the best air fryer ovens I have used to date that meets all my cooking requirements. I depend much on Kalorik Air Fryer to meet my busy schedules, and the air fryer has always been a savior to take care of my family's food requirements. I am content with its multipurpose functions and loved cooking with it. The air fryer can cook 30% faster than any other contemporary air fryer appliance. Its performance reiterates the tagline of '30% faster cooking,' which I can underline from my personal experience. Thanks to the 1700 watts turbo MAXX airflow technology for making the cooking much faster.

The turbo airflow technology can increase the inner chamber temperature to 500 Fahrenheit within a short period. As a result, it can cook the food 50% faster than any ordinary air fryer ovens. The air fryer takes a maximum of 40 minutes for cooking, and while the cooking is in progress, you can open the door to flip the food occasionally to get it cooked evenly on both sides. The faster way of cooking does not spoil the quality and crispiness of the food; instead, it reduces the fat and calories.

Automatic Shutdown Feature

The appliance comes with a French glass double door that resists any dripping and scalding on the oven doors. The doors can open with single hand and comes with handles mounted on the front side, making it convenient to place the food in and take it out from the oven. It gives a modern touch to your cooking with these advanced air frying features. For additional safety, the cooking process can control by the timer and an automatic shut off feature. The appliance will shut down automatically when the door is open.

Spacious, Spacious, Spacious

The air fryer oven is quite spacious with a capacity of 26 quarters, which outsmart the competitors. In its sizeable cooking chamber, you can cook food for a whole family in a single go. You can even roast a whole chicken, and it can air fry 12" pizza, 9 slices of bread, and besides, it still has space for frying other dishes while the primary cooking is underway.

Body Construction and Cleaning

Kalorik comes with a stainless steel body, and it is lightweight; therefore, the appliance is easy to move to any location for cooking. Its compact design is another advantage, and hence, it consumes less space as well. I also felt the air fryer oven fan is a lot quieter than other ovens but keeps rotating even after the cooking is over to cool the machine. The parts inside the air fryer oven are removable, making it easy for maintenance and cleaning.

Read the Owner's Manual.

You will get a proper understanding of using the machine without any trouble by going through the owner's manual. The manual also offers various tips and safety instructions to adhere to while the appliance is working. Along with the owner's manual, you will also get a cookbook with 40 mouth-watering recipes.

Experience a New Way of Cooking

Experiment with new recipes and give your food a professional restaurant touch. You can cook like a professional chef by following the step-by-step cooking directions. The cookbook is informative, and it also provides the nutritional values of each recipe. Since I have been using it for a long time, I can confidently recommend Kalorik Maxx to my readers.

You don't need to be an expert in cooking or require technical knowledge to use this air fryer. The cookbook and instruction manual have every essential tips and instruction for using the appliance. You just have to follow the cooking time and sequences.

Easy Settings and Maintenance

With Kalorik, you don't have to spend too much time on cooking. You can use the selector button to preset the time and temperature in the LED display by rotating the dial knob. Apart from that, it has features for rotisserie rotating, a light button where you can turn on or off the light anytime, an air fry button, an oven button, and finally, the start/stop button. The detailed instruction manual has everything you want to know about the air fryer oven's settings and functions. Unlike some other air fryer ovens, Kalorik won't exert heat and fill the kitchen with a cooking smell.

Cleaning

Since the air fryer uses high-quality stainless steel, you will find cleaning is a hassle-free experience. Its accessories are with nonstick coated stainless-steel material, making it easy to clean. You can clean the accessories by scrubbing in soap water to remove the stains and sticky foods. Make sure to wipe the whole interior of the air fryer oven before using it again, and wait until it becomes dry to start the new cooking.

How to Ease Up the Cooking

Reading the manual and recipe is a paramount factor in understanding the air fryer and its utilities. Before start cooking, collect all the ingredients, and keep it handy. Wash all the vegetables/non-veg items before cooking and follow the instruction for the preparation. Once all the ingredients and cookware are ready, you can start cooking as per the cooking directions. The process will let you enjoy cooking.

Make cooking a fun-filled activity by applying your heart and soul to the actions. A positive attitude and openness to learning new culinary techniques will let you enjoy the cooking. If you can cook happily, then the kitchen will be your favorite place for leisure and enjoyment. Having a Kalorik Maxx Air Fryer Oven in the kitchen can take you to a new cooking level. The air fryer will set a new level of kitchen ambiance. To break the mundane cooking experience, I suggest you try different recipes.

Final Thoughts

If you have a Kalorik Maxx Air Fryer Oven in the kitchen, there is no need to compromise your busy working schedules to cook healthy foods. The air fryer oven won't consume much of your time, as the foods can get cooked within 40 minutes maximum. The Kalorik air fryer would impress you with its price; it is one of the most affordable high-tech ovens with innovative features incorporated to bring better results.

Don't you think it is the time to show off your cooking skills and create an impression on others? Wait no more and prepare food like a pro. Make every mealtime a lot more special with a Kalorik Maxx Air Fryer Oven by trying the cookbook's delicious recipes.

Chapter 1

Breakfasts

Lush Vegetable Omelet

Prep time: 10 minutes | Cook time: 13 minutes | Serves 2

- 2 teaspoons canola oil
- 4 eggs, whisked
- 3 tablespoons plain milk
- 1 teaspoon melted butter
- 1 red bell pepper, seeded and chopped
- 1 green bell pepper, seeded and chopped
- 1 white onion, finely chopped
- ½ cup baby spinach leaves, roughly chopped
- ½ cup Halloumi cheese, shaved
- Kosher salt and freshly ground black pepper, to taste

1. Select the BAKE function and preheat MAXX to 350ºF (177ºC).
2. Grease a baking pan with canola oil.
3. Put the remaining ingredients in the baking pan and stir well.
4. Transfer to the air fryer oven and bake for 13 minutes.
5. Serve warm.

Ham and Corn Muffins

Prep time: 10 minutes | Cook time: 6 minutes | Makes 8 muffins

- ¾ cup yellow cornmeal
- ¼ cup flour
- 1½ teaspoons baking powder
- ¼ teaspoon salt
- 1 egg, beaten
- 2 tablespoons canola oil
- ½ cup milk
- ½ cup shredded sharp Cheddar cheese
- ½ cup diced ham

1. Select the BAKE function and preheat MAXX to 390ºF (199ºC).
2. In a medium bowl, stir together the cornmeal, flour, baking powder, and salt.
3. Add the egg, oil, and milk to dry ingredients and mix well.
4. Stir in shredded cheese and diced ham.
5. Divide batter among 8 parchment paper-lined muffin cups.
6. Put 4 filled muffin cups in air fryer basket and bake for 5 minutes.
7. Reduce temperature to 330ºF (166ºC) and bake for 1 minute or until a toothpick inserted in center of the muffin comes out clean.
8. Repeat with the remaining muffins.
9. Serve warm.

Spinach with Scrambled Eggs

Prep time: 10 minutes | Cook time: 10 minutes | Serves 2

- 2 tablespoons olive oil
- 4 eggs, whisked
- 5 ounces (142 g) fresh spinach, chopped
- 1 medium tomato, chopped
- 1 teaspoon fresh lemon juice
- ½ teaspoon coarse salt
- ½ teaspoon ground black pepper
- ½ cup of fresh basil, roughly chopped

1. Grease a baking pan with the oil, tilting it to spread the oil around. Select the BAKE function and preheat MAXX to 280ºF (138ºC).
2. Mix the remaining ingredients, apart from the basil leaves, whisking well until everything is completely combined.
3. Bake in the air fryer oven for 10 minutes.
4. Top with fresh basil leaves before serving.

Soufflé

Prep time: 10 minutes | Cook time: 22 minutes | Serves 4

- ⅓ cup butter, melted
- ¼ cup flour
- 1 cup milk
- 1 ounce (28 g) sugar
- 4 egg yolks
- 1 teaspoon vanilla extract
- 6 egg whites
- 1 teaspoon cream of tartar
- Cooking spray

1. In a bowl, mix the butter and flour until a smooth consistency is achieved.
2. Pour the milk into a saucepan over medium-low heat. Add the sugar and allow to dissolve before raising the heat to boil the milk.
3. Pour in the flour and butter mixture and stir rigorously for 7 minutes to eliminate any lumps. Make sure the mixture thickens. Take off the heat and allow to cool for 15 minutes.
4. Select the BAKE function and preheat MAXX to 320ºF (160ºC). Spritz 6 soufflé dishes with cooking spray.
5. Put the egg yolks and vanilla extract in a separate bowl and beat them together with a fork. Pour in the milk and combine well to incorporate everything.
6. In a smaller bowl mix the egg whites and cream of tartar with a fork. Fold into the egg yolks-milk mixture before adding in the flour mixture. Transfer equal amounts to the 6 soufflé dishes.
7. Put the dishes in the air fryer oven and bake for 15 minutes.
8. Serve warm.

Fast Coffee Donuts

Prep time: 5 minutes | Cook time: 6 minutes | Serves 6

- ¼ cup sugar
- ½ teaspoon salt
- 1 cup flour
- 1 teaspoon baking powder
- ¼ cup coffee
- 1 tablespoon aquafaba
- 1 tablespoon sunflower oil

1. In a large bowl, combine the sugar, salt, flour, and baking powder.
2. Add the coffee, aquafaba, and sunflower oil and mix until a dough is formed. Leave the dough to rest in and the refrigerator.
3. Remove the dough from the fridge and divide up, kneading each section into a doughnut.
4. Put the doughnuts inside the air fryer oven. Select the AIR FRY function and cook at 400ºF (204ºC) for 6 minutes.
5. Serve immediately.

Mushroom and Squash Toast

Prep time: 10 minutes | Cook time: 10 minutes | Serves 4

- 1 tablespoon olive oil
- 1 red bell pepper, cut into strips
- 2 green onions, sliced
- 1 cup sliced button or cremini mushrooms
- 1 small yellow squash, sliced
- 2 tablespoons softened butter
- 4 slices bread
- ½ cup soft goat cheese

1. Brush the air fryer basket with the olive oil.
2. Put the red pepper, green onions, mushrooms, and squash inside the air fryer oven and give them a stir. Select the AIR FRY function and cook at 350ºF (177ºC) for 7 minutes, or until the vegetables are tender, shaking the basket once throughout the cooking time.
3. Remove the vegetables and set them aside.
4. Spread the butter on the slices of bread and transfer to the air fryer oven, butter-side up. Brown for 3 minutes.
5. Remove the toast from the air fryer oven and top with goat cheese and vegetables. Serve warm.

Creamy Cinnamon Rolls

Prep time: 10 minutes | Cook time: 9 minutes | Serves 8

- 1 pound (454 g) frozen bread dough, thawed
- ¼ cup butter, melted
- ¾ cup brown sugar
- 1½ tablespoons ground cinnamon
- Cream Cheese Glaze:
- 4 ounces (113 g) cream cheese, softened
- 2 tablespoons butter, softened
- 1¼ cups powdered sugar
- ½ teaspoon vanilla extract

1. Let the bread dough come to room temperature on the counter. On a lightly floured surface, roll the dough into a 13-inch by 11-inch rectangle. Position the rectangle so the 13-inch side is facing you. Brush the melted butter all over the dough, leaving a 1-inch border uncovered along the edge farthest away from you.
2. Combine the brown sugar and cinnamon in a small bowl. Sprinkle the mixture evenly over the buttered dough, keeping the 1-inch border uncovered. Roll the dough into a log, starting with the edge closest to you. Roll the dough tightly, rolling evenly, and push out any air pockets. When you get to the uncovered edge of the dough, press the dough onto the roll to seal it together.
3. Cut the log into 8 pieces, slicing slowly with a sawing motion so you don't flatten the dough. Turn the slices on their sides and cover with a clean kitchen towel. Let the rolls sit in the warmest part of the kitchen for 1½ to 2 hours to rise.
4. To make the glaze, place the cream cheese and butter in a microwave-safe bowl. Soften the mixture in the microwave for 30 seconds at a time until it is easy to stir. Gradually add the powdered sugar and stir to combine. Add the vanilla extract and whisk until smooth. Set aside.
5. When the rolls have risen, transfer 4 of the rolls to the air fryer basket. Select the AIR FRY function and cook at 350ºF (177ºC) for 5 minutes. Turn the rolls over and air fry for another 4 minutes. Repeat with the remaining 4 rolls.
6. Let the rolls cool for two minutes before glazing. Spread large dollops of cream cheese glaze on top of the warm cinnamon rolls, allowing some glaze to drip down the side of the rolls. Serve warm.

Potato Bread Rolls

Prep time: 15 minutes | Cook time: 20 minutes | Serves 5

- 5 large potatoes, boiled and mashed
- Salt and ground black pepper, to taste
- ½ teaspoon mustard seeds
- 1 tablespoon olive oil
- 2 small onions, chopped
- 2 sprigs curry leaves
- ½ teaspoon turmeric powder
- 2 green chilis, seeded and chopped
- 1 bunch coriander, chopped
- 8 slices bread, brown sides discarded

1. Put the mashed potatoes in a bowl and sprinkle on salt and pepper. Set to one side.
2. Fry the mustard seeds in olive oil over a medium-low heat in a skillet, stirring continuously, until they sputter.
3. Add the onions and cook until they turn translucent. Add the curry leaves and turmeric powder and stir. Cook for a further 2 minutes until fragrant.
4. Remove the pan from the heat and combine with the potatoes. Mix in the green chilies and coriander.
5. Wet the bread slightly and drain of any excess liquid.
6. Spoon a small amount of the potato mixture into the center of the bread and enclose the bread around the filling, sealing it entirely. Continue until the rest of the bread and filling is used up. Brush each bread roll with some oil and transfer to the air fryer basket.
7. Select the AIR FRY function and cook at 400ºF (204ºC) for 15 minutes, gently shaking the air fryer basket at the halfway point to ensure each roll is cooked evenly.
8. Serve immediately.

Chapter 2

Vegetables

Simple Pesto Gnocchi

Prep time: 10 minutes | Cook time: 15 minutes | Serves 4

- 1 (1-pound / 454-g) package gnocchi
- 1 medium onion, chopped
- 3 cloves garlic, minced
- 1 tablespoon extra-virgin olive oil
- 1 (8-ounce / 227-g) jar pesto
- 1/3 cup grated Parmesan cheese

1. In a large bowl combine the onion, garlic, and gnocchi, and drizzle with the olive oil. Mix thoroughly.
2. Transfer the mixture to the air fryer oven. Select the AIR FRY function and cook at 340ºF (171ºC) for 15 minutes, stirring occasionally, making sure the gnocchi become light brown and crispy.
3. Add the pesto and Parmesan cheese, and give everything a good stir before serving.

Golden Pickles

Prep time: 10 minutes | Cook time: 15 minutes | Serves 4

- 14 dill pickles, sliced
- ¼ cup flour
- ⅛ teaspoon baking powder
- Pinch of salt
- 2 tablespoons cornstarch plus 3
- tablespoons water
- 6 tablespoons panko bread crumbs
- ½ teaspoon paprika
- Cooking spray

1. Drain any excess moisture out of the dill pickles on a paper towel.
2. In a bowl, combine the flour, baking powder and salt.
3. Throw in the cornstarch and water mixture and combine well with a whisk.
4. Put the panko bread crumbs in a shallow dish along with the paprika. Mix thoroughly.
5. Dip the pickles in the flour batter, before coating in the bread crumbs. Spritz all the pickles with the cooking spray.
6. Transfer to the air fryer basket. Select the AIR FRY function and cook at 400ºF (204ºC) for 15 minutes, or until golden brown.
7. Serve immediately.

Lemony Falafel

Prep time: 15 minutes | Cook time: 15 minutes | Serves 8

- 1 teaspoon cumin seeds
- ½ teaspoon coriander seeds
- 2 cups chickpeas, drained and rinsed
- ½ teaspoon red pepper flakes
- 3 cloves garlic
- ¼ cup chopped parsley
- ¼ cup chopped coriander
- ½ onion, diced
- 1 tablespoon juice from freshly squeezed lemon
- 3 tablespoons flour
- ½ teaspoon salt
- Cooking spray

1. Fry the cumin and coriander seeds over medium heat until fragrant.
2. Grind using a mortar and pestle.
3. Put all of ingredients, except for the cooking spray, in a food processor and blend until a fine consistency is achieved.
4. Use the hands to mold the mixture into falafels and spritz with the cooking spray.
5. Transfer the falafels to the air fryer basket in one layer.
6. Select the AIR FRY function and cook at 400ºF (204ºC) for 15 minutes, serving when they turn golden brown.

Roasted Lemony Broccoli

Prep time: 5 minutes | Cook time: 15 minutes | Serves 6

- 2 heads broccoli, cut into florets
- 2 teaspoons extra-virgin olive oil, plus more for coating
- 1 teaspoon salt
- ½ teaspoon black pepper
- 1 clove garlic, minced
- ½ teaspoon lemon juice

1. Cover the air fryer basket with aluminum foil and coat with a light brushing of oil.
2. Select the ROAST function and preheat MAXX to 375ºF (191ºC).
3. In a bowl, combine all ingredients, save for the lemon juice, and transfer to the air fryer basket. Roast for 15 minutes.
4. Serve with the lemon juice.

Cheesy Macaroni Balls

Prep time: 10 minutes | Cook time: 10 minutes | Serves 2

- 2 cups leftover macaroni
- 1 cup shredded Cheddar cheese
- ½ cup flour
- 1 cup bread crumbs
- 3 large eggs
- 1 cup milk
- ½ teaspoon salt
- ¼ teaspoon black pepper

1. In a bowl, combine the leftover macaroni and shredded cheese.
2. Pour the flour in a separate bowl. Put the bread crumbs in a third bowl. Finally, in a fourth bowl, mix the eggs and milk with a whisk.
3. With an ice-cream scoop, create balls from the macaroni mixture. Coat them the flour, then in the egg mixture, and lastly in the bread crumbs.
4. Arrange the balls in the air fryer basket. Select the AIR FRY function and cook at 365ºF (185ºC) for 10 minutes, giving them an occasional stir. Ensure they crisp up nicely.
5. Serve hot.

Corn Pakodas

Prep time: 10 minutes | Cook time: 8 minutes | Serves 5

- 1 cup flour
- ¼ teaspoon baking soda
- ¼ teaspoon salt
- ½ teaspoon curry powder
- ½ teaspoon red chili powder
- ¼ teaspoon turmeric powder
- ¼ cup water
- 10 cobs baby corn, blanched
- Cooking spray

1. Cover the air fryer basket with aluminum foil and spritz with the cooking spray.
2. In a bowl, combine all the ingredients, save for the corn. Stir with a whisk until well combined.
3. Coat the corn in the batter and put inside the air fryer oven.
4. Select the AIR FRY function and cook at 425ºF (218ºC) for 8 minutes, or until a golden brown color is achieved.
5. Serve hot.

Jalapeño Poppers

Prep time: 5 minutes | Cook time: 33 minutes
Serves 4

Stuffed Vegetables

- 8 medium jalapeño peppers
- 5 ounces (142 g) cream cheese
- ¼ cup grated Mozzarella cheese
- ½ teaspoon Italian seasoning mix
- 8 slices bacon

1. Select the BAKE function and preheat MAXX to 400ºF (204ºC).
2. Cut the jalapeños in half.
3. Use a spoon to scrape out the insides of the peppers.
4. In a bowl, add together the cream cheese, Mozzarella cheese and Italian seasoning.
5. Pack the cream cheese mixture into the jalapeño halves and place the other halves on top.
6. Wrap each pepper in 1 slice of bacon, starting from the bottom and working up.
7. Bake for 33 minutes.
8. Serve!

Golden Garlicky Mushrooms

Prep time: 10 minutes | Cook time: 10 minutes | Serves 4

- 6 small mushrooms
- 1 tablespoon bread crumbs
- 1 tablespoon olive oil
- 1 ounce (28 g) onion, peeled and diced
- 1 teaspoon parsley
- 1 teaspoon garlic purée
- Salt and ground black pepper, to taste

1. Combine the bread crumbs, oil, onion, parsley, salt, pepper and garlic in a bowl. Cut out the mushrooms' stalks and stuff each cap with the crumb mixture.
2. Select the AIR FRY function and cook the mushrooms in the air fryer oven at 350ºF (177ºC) for 10 minutes.
3. Serve hot.

Ricotta Potatoes

Prep time: 15 minutes | Cook time: 15 minutes | Serves 4

- 4 potatoes
- 2 tablespoons olive oil
- ½ cup Ricotta cheese, at room temperature
- 2 tablespoons chopped scallions
- 1 tablespoon roughly chopped fresh parsley
- 1 tablespoon minced coriander
- 2 ounces (57 g) Cheddar cheese, preferably freshly grated
- 1 teaspoon celery seeds
- ½ teaspoon salt
- ½ teaspoon garlic pepper

1. Pierce the skin of the potatoes with a knife. Transfer to the air fryer basket.
2. Select the AIR FRY function and cook at 350ºF (177ºC) for 13 minutes. If they are not cooked through by this time, leave for 2 to 3 minutes longer.
3. In the meantime, make the stuffing by combining all the other ingredients.
4. Cut halfway into the cooked potatoes to open them.
5. Spoon equal amounts of the stuffing into each potato and serve hot.

Kidney Beans Oatmeal in Peppers

Prep time: 15 minutes | Cook time: 6 minutes | Serves 2 to 4

- 2 large bell peppers, halved lengthwise, deseeded
- 2 tablespoons cooked kidney beans
- 2 tablespoons cooked chick peas
- 2 cups cooked oatmeal
- 1 teaspoon ground cumin
- ½ teaspoon paprika
- ½ teaspoon salt or to taste
- ¼ teaspoon black pepper powder
- ¼ cup yogurt

1. Put the bell peppers, cut-side down, in the air fryer basket. Select the AIR FRY function and cook at 355ºF (179ºC) for 2 minutes.
2. Take the peppers out of the air fryer oven and let cool.
3. In a bowl, combine the rest of the ingredients.
4. Divide the mixture evenly and use each portion to stuff a pepper.
5. Return the stuffed peppers to the air fryer oven and continue to air fry for 4 minutes.
6. Serve hot.

Gorgonzola Mushrooms with Horseradish Mayo

Prep time: 15 minutes | Cook time: 10 minutes | Serves 5

- ½ cup bread crumbs
- 2 cloves garlic, pressed
- 2 tablespoons chopped fresh coriander
- $1/_3$ teaspoon kosher salt
- ½ teaspoon crushed red pepper flakes
- 1½ tablespoons olive oil
- 20 medium mushrooms, stems removed
- ½ cup grated Gorgonzola cheese
- ¼ cup low-fat mayonnaise
- 1 teaspoon prepared horseradish, well-drained
- 1 tablespoon finely chopped fresh parsley

1. Combine the bread crumbs together with the garlic, coriander, salt, red pepper, and olive oil.
2. Take equal-sized amounts of the bread crumb mixture and use them to stuff the mushroom caps. Add the grated Gorgonzola on top of each.
3. Put the mushrooms in a baking pan and transfer to the air fryer oven.
4. Select the AIR FRY function and cook at 380ºF (193ºC) for 10 minutes, ensuring the stuffing is warm throughout.
5. In the meantime, prepare the horseradish mayo. Mix the mayonnaise, horseradish and parsley.
6. When the mushrooms are ready, serve with the mayo.

Marinara Pepperoni Mushroom Pizza

Prep time: 5 minutes | Cook time: 18 minutes | Serves 4

- 4 large portobello mushrooms, stems removed
- 4 teaspoons olive oil
- 1 cup marinara sauce
- 1 cup shredded Mozzarella cheese
- 10 slices sugar-free pepperoni

1. Select the BAKE function and preheat MAXX to 375ºF (191ºC).
2. Brush each mushroom cap with the olive oil, one teaspoon for each cap.
3. Put on a baking sheet and bake, stem-side down, for 8 minutes.
4. Take out of the air fryer oven and divide the marinara sauce, Mozzarella cheese and pepperoni evenly among the caps.
5. Switch from BAKE to AIR FRY. Air fry for another 10 minutes until browned.
6. Serve hot.

Chapter 3

Fish and Seafood

Spicy Orange Shrimp

Prep time: 20 minutes | Cook time: 10 to 15 minutes | Serves 4

- ⅓ cup orange juice
- 3 teaspoons minced garlic
- 1 teaspoon Old Bay seasoning
- ¼ to ½ teaspoon cayenne pepper
- 1 pound (454 g) medium shrimp, peeled and deveined, with tails off
- Cooking spray

1. In a medium bowl, combine the orange juice, garlic, Old Bay seasoning, and cayenne pepper.
2. Dry the shrimp with paper towels to remove excess water.
3. Add the shrimp to the marinade and stir to evenly coat. Cover with plastic wrap and place in the refrigerator for 30 minutes so the shrimp can soak up the marinade.
4. Spray the air fryer basket lightly with cooking spray.
5. Place the shrimp into the air fryer basket. Select the AIR FRY function and cook at 400ºF (204ºC) for 5 minutes. Shake the basket and lightly spray with olive oil. Air fry until the shrimp are opaque and crisp, 5 to 10 more minutes.
6. Serve immediately.

Blackened Shrimp Tacos

Prep time: 10 minutes | Cook time: 10 to 15 minutes | Serves 4

- 12 ounces (340 g) medium shrimp, deveined, with tails off
- 1 teaspoon olive oil
- 1 to 2 teaspoons Blackened seasoning
- 8 corn tortillas, warmed
- 1 (14-ounce / 397-g) bag coleslaw mix
- 2 limes, cut in half
- Cooking spray

1. Spray the air fryer basket lightly with cooking spray.
2. Dry the shrimp with a paper towel to remove excess water.
3. In a medium bowl, toss the shrimp with olive oil and Blackened seasoning.
4. Place the shrimp in the air fryer basket. Select the AIR FRY function and cook at 400ºF (204ºC) for 5 minutes. Shake the basket, lightly spray with cooking spray, and cook until the shrimp are cooked through and starting to brown, 5 to 10 more minutes.
5. Fill each tortilla with the coleslaw mix and top with the blackened shrimp. Squeeze fresh lime juice over top and serve.

Spanish Garlic Shrimp

Prep time: 10 minutes | Cook time: 10 to 15 minutes | Serves 4

- 2 teaspoons minced garlic
- 2 teaspoons lemon juice
- 2 teaspoons olive oil
- ½ to 1 teaspoon crushed red

- pepper
- 12 ounces (340 g) medium shrimp, deveined, with tails on
- Cooking spray

1. In a medium bowl, mix together the garlic, lemon juice, olive oil, and crushed red pepper to make a marinade.
2. Add the shrimp and toss to coat in the marinade. Cover with plastic wrap and place the bowl in the refrigerator for 30 minutes.
3. Spray the air fryer basket lightly with cooking spray. Place the shrimp in the air fryer basket.
4. Select the AIR FRY function and cook at 400ºF (204ºC) for 5 minutes. Shake the basket and air fry until the shrimp are cooked through and nicely browned, an additional 5 to 10 minutes.
5. Cool for 5 minutes before serving.

Garlic Scallops

Prep time: 10 minutes | Cook time: 10 to 15 minutes | Serves 4

- 2 teaspoons olive oil
- 1 packet dry zesty Italian dressing mix
- 1 teaspoon minced garlic

- 16 ounces (454 g) small scallops, patted dry
- Cooking spray

1. Spray the air fryer basket lightly with cooking spray.
2. In a large zip-top plastic bag, combine the olive oil, Italian dressing mix, and garlic.
3. Add the scallops, seal the zip-top bag, and coat the scallops in the seasoning mixture.
4. Place the scallops in the air fryer basket and lightly spray with cooking spray.
5. Select the AIR FRY function and cook at 400ºF (204ºC) for 5 minutes. Shake the basket, and air fry for 5 to 10 more minutes, or until the scallops reach an internal temperature of 120ºF (49ºC).
6. Serve immediately.

Garlic-Lemon Tilapia

Prep time: 5 minutes | Cook time: 10 to 15 minutes | Serves 4

- 1 tablespoon lemon juice
- 1 tablespoon olive oil
- 1 teaspoon minced garlic
- ½ teaspoon chili powder
- 4 (6-ounce / 170-g) tilapia fillets

1. Line the air fryer basket with parchment paper.
2. In a large, shallow bowl, mix together the lemon juice, olive oil, garlic, and chili powder to make a marinade. Place the tilapia fillets in the bowl and coat evenly.
3. Place the fillets in the basket in a single layer, leaving space between each fillet. You may need to cook in more than one batch.
4. Select the AIR FRY function and cook at 380ºF (193ºC) for 10 to 15 minutes, or until the fish is cooked and flakes easily with a fork.
5. Serve hot.

Lime-Chili Shrimp Bowl

Prep time: 10 minutes | Cook time: 10 to 15 minutes | Serves 4

- 2 teaspoons lime juice
- 1 teaspoon olive oil
- 1 teaspoon honey
- 1 teaspoon minced garlic
- 1 teaspoon chili powder
- Salt, to taste
- 12 ounces (340 g) medium shrimp,
- peeled and deveined
- 2 cups cooked brown rice
- 1 (15-ounce / 425-g) can seasoned black beans, warmed
- 1 large avocado, chopped
- 1 cup sliced cherry tomatoes
- Cooking spray

1. Spray the air fryer basket lightly with cooking spray.
2. In a medium bowl, mix together the lime juice, olive oil, honey, garlic, chili powder, and salt to make a marinade.
3. Add the shrimp and toss to coat evenly in the marinade.
4. Place the shrimp in the air fryer basket. Select the AIR FRY function and cook at 400ºF (204ºC) for 5 minutes. Shake the basket and air fry until the shrimp are cooked through and starting to brown, an additional 5 to 10 minutes.
5. To assemble the bowls, spoon ¼ of the rice, black beans, avocado, and cherry tomatoes into each of four bowls. Top with the shrimp and serve.

Green Curry Shrimp

Prep time: 15 minutes | Cook time: 5 minutes | Serves 4

- 1 to 2 tablespoons Thai green curry paste
- 2 tablespoons coconut oil, melted
- 1 tablespoon half-and-half or coconut milk
- 1 teaspoon fish sauce
- 1 teaspoon soy sauce

- 1 teaspoon minced fresh ginger
- 1 clove garlic, minced
- 1 pound (454 g) jumbo raw shrimp, peeled and deveined
- ¼ cup chopped fresh Thai basil or sweet basil
- ¼ cup chopped fresh cilantro

1. In a baking pan, combine the curry paste, coconut oil, half-and-half, fish sauce, soy sauce, ginger, and garlic. Whisk until well combined.
2. Add the shrimp and toss until well coated. Marinate at room temperature for 15 to 30 minutes.
3. Place the pan in the air fryer basket. Select the AIR FRY function and cook at 400ºF (204ºC) for 5 minutes, stirring halfway through the cooking time.
4. Transfer the shrimp to a serving bowl or platter. Garnish with the basil and cilantro. Serve immediately.

Tuna Patty Sliders

Prep time: 15 minutes | Cook time: 10 to 15 minutes | Serves 4

- 3 (5-ounce / 142-g) cans tuna, packed in water
- ⅔ cup whole-wheat panko bread crumbs
- ⅓ cup shredded Parmesan cheese

- 1 tablespoon sriracha
- ¾ teaspoon black pepper
- 10 whole-wheat slider buns
- Cooking spray

1. Spray the air fryer basket lightly with cooking spray.
2. In a medium bowl combine the tuna, bread crumbs, Parmesan cheese, sriracha, and black pepper and stir to combine.
3. Form the mixture into 10 patties.
4. Place the patties in the air fryer basket in a single layer. Spray the patties lightly with cooking spray. You may need to cook them in batches.
5. Select the AIR FRY function and cook at 350ºF (177ºC) for 6 to 8 minutes. Turn the patties over and lightly spray with cooking spray. Air fry until golden brown and crisp, another 4 to 7 more minutes. Serve warm.

Crispy Catfish Strips

Prep time: 5 minutes | Cook time: 16 to 18 minutes | Serves 4

- 1 cup buttermilk
- 5 catfish fillets, cut into 1½-inch strips
- Cooking spray
- 1 cup cornmeal
- 1 tablespoon Creole, Cajun, or Old Bay seasoning

1. Pour the buttermilk into a shallow baking dish. Place the catfish in the dish and refrigerate for at least 1 hour to help remove any fishy taste.
2. Spray the air fryer basket lightly with cooking spray.
3. In a shallow bowl, combine cornmeal and Creole seasoning.
4. Shake any excess buttermilk off the catfish. Place each strip in the cornmeal mixture and coat completely. Press the cornmeal into the catfish gently to help it stick.
5. Place the strips in the air fryer basket in a single layer. Lightly spray the catfish with cooking spray. You may need to cook the catfish in more than one batch.
6. Select the AIR FRY function and cook at 400°F (204°C) for 8 minutes. Turn the catfish strips over and lightly spray with cooking spray. Air fry until golden brown and crispy, 8 to 10 more minutes.
7. Serve warm.

Seasoned Breaded Shrimp

Prep time: 15 minutes | Cook time: 10 to 15 minutes | Serves 4

- 2 teaspoons Old Bay seasoning, divided
- ½ teaspoon garlic powder
- ½ teaspoon onion powder
- 1 pound (454 g) large shrimp,
- deveined, with tails on
- 2 large eggs
- ½ cup whole-wheat panko bread crumbs
- Cooking spray

1. Spray the air fryer basket lightly with cooking spray.
2. In a medium bowl, mix together 1 teaspoon of Old Bay seasoning, garlic powder, and onion powder. Add the shrimp and toss with the seasoning mix to lightly coat.
3. In a separate small bowl, whisk the eggs with 1 teaspoon water.
4. In a shallow bowl, mix together the remaining 1 teaspoon Old Bay seasoning and the panko bread crumbs.

5. Dip each shrimp in the egg mixture and dredge in the bread crumb mixture to evenly coat.
6. Place the shrimp in the air fryer basket, in a single layer. Lightly spray the shrimp with cooking spray. You many need to cook the shrimp in batches.
7. Select the AIR FRY function and cook at 380ºF (193ºC) for 10 to 15 minutes, or until the shrimp is cooked through and crispy, shaking the basket at 5-minute intervals to redistribute and evenly cook.
8. Serve immediately.

Homemade Fish Sticks

Prep time: 15 minutes | Cook time: 10 to 15 minutes | Serves 4

- 4 fish fillets
- ½ cup whole-wheat flour
- 1 teaspoon seasoned salt
- 2 eggs
- 1½ cups whole-wheat panko bread crumbs
- ½ tablespoon dried parsley flakes
- Cooking spray

1. Spray the air fryer basket lightly with cooking spray.
2. Cut the fish fillets lengthwise into "sticks."
3. In a shallow bowl, mix the whole-wheat flour and seasoned salt.
4. In a small bowl, whisk the eggs with 1 teaspoon of water.
5. In another shallow bowl, mix the panko bread crumbs and parsley flakes.
6. Coat each fish stick in the seasoned flour, then in the egg mixture, and dredge them in the panko bread crumbs.
7. Place the fish sticks in the air fryer basket in a single layer and lightly spray the fish sticks with cooking spray. You may need to cook them in batches.
8. Select the AIR FRY function and cook at 400ºF (204ºC) for 5 to 8 minutes. Flip the fish sticks over and lightly spray with the cooking spray. Air fry until golden brown and crispy, 5 to 7 more minutes.
9. Serve warm.

Air Fried Spring Rolls

Prep time: 10 minutes | Cook time: 17 to 22 minutes | Serves 4

- 2 teaspoons minced garlic
- 2 cups finely sliced cabbage
- 1 cup matchstick cut carrots
- 2 (4-ounce / 113-g) cans tiny shrimp, drained
- 4 teaspoons soy sauce
- Salt and freshly ground black pepper, to taste
- 16 square spring roll wrappers
- Cooking spray

1. Spray the air fryer basket lightly with cooking spray. Spray a medium sauté pan with cooking spray.
2. Add the garlic to the sauté pan and cook over medium heat until fragrant, 30 to 45 seconds. Add the cabbage and carrots and sauté until the vegetables are slightly tender, about 5 minutes.
3. Add the shrimp and soy sauce and season with salt and pepper, then stir to combine. Sauté until the moisture has evaporated, 2 more minutes. Set aside to cool.
4. Place a spring roll wrapper on a work surface so it looks like a diamond. Place 1 tablespoon of the shrimp mixture on the lower end of the wrapper.
5. Roll the wrapper away from you halfway, then fold in the right and left sides, like an envelope. Continue to roll to the very end, using a little water to seal the edge. Repeat with the remaining wrappers and filling.
6. Place the spring rolls in the air fryer basket in a single layer, leaving room between each roll. Lightly spray with cooking spray. You may need to cook them in batches.
7. Select the AIR FRY function and cook at 370ºF (188ºC) for 5 minutes. Turn the rolls over, lightly spray with cooking spray, and air fry until heated through and the rolls start to brown, 5 to 10 more minutes. Cool for 5 minutes before serving.

Salmon Burgers

Prep time: 15 minutes | Cook time: 12 minutes | Serves 5

Lemon-Caper Rémoulade:
- ½ cup mayonnaise
- 2 tablespoons minced drained capers
- 2 tablespoons chopped fresh parsley
- 2 teaspoons fresh lemon juice

Salmon Patties:
- 1 pound (454 g) wild salmon fillet, skinned and pin bones removed
- 6 tablespoons panko bread crumbs
- ¼ cup minced red onion plus ¼ cup slivered for serving
- 1 garlic clove, minced
- 1 large egg, lightly beaten
- 1 tablespoon Dijon mustard
- 1 teaspoon fresh lemon juice
- 1 tablespoon chopped fresh parsley
- ½ teaspoon kosher salt

For Serving:
- 5 whole wheat potato buns or gluten-free buns
- 10 butter lettuce leaves

1. For the lemon-caper rémoulade: In a small bowl, combine the mayonnaise, capers, parsley, and lemon juice and mix well.
2. For the salmon patties: Cut off a 4-ounce / 113-g piece of the salmon and transfer to a food processor. Pulse until it becomes pasty. With a sharp knife, chop the remaining salmon into small cubes.
3. In a medium bowl, combine the chopped and processed salmon with the panko, minced red onion, garlic, egg, mustard, lemon juice, parsley, and salt. Toss gently to combine. Form the mixture into 5 patties about ¾ inch thick. Refrigerate for at least 30 minutes.
4. Working in batches, place the patties in the air fryer basket. Select the AIR FRY function and cook at 400ºF (204ºC) for 12 minutes, gently flipping halfway, until golden and cooked through.
5. To serve, transfer each patty to a bun. Top each with 2 lettuce leaves, 2 tablespoons of the rémoulade, and the slivered red onions.

Chapter 4

Poultry

Fajita Chicken Strips

Prep time: 10 minutes | Cook time: 15 minutes | Serves 4

- 1 pound (454 g) boneless, skinless chicken tenderloins, cut into strips
- 3 bell peppers, any color, cut into chunks
- 1 onion, cut into chunks
- 1 tablespoon olive oil
- 1 tablespoon fajita seasoning mix
- Cooking spray

1. In a large bowl, mix together the chicken, bell peppers, onion, olive oil, and fajita seasoning mix until completely coated.
2. Spray the air fryer basket lightly with cooking spray.
3. Place the chicken and vegetables in the air fryer basket and lightly spray with cooking spray.
4. Select the AIR FRY function and cook at 370ºF (188ºC) for 7 minutes. Shake the basket and air fry for an additional 5 to 8 minutes, until the chicken is cooked through and the veggies are starting to char.
5. Serve warm.

Sweet-and-Sour Drumsticks

Prep time: 5 minutes | Cook time: 23 to 25 minutes | Serves 4

- 6 chicken drumsticks
- 3 tablespoons lemon juice, divided
- 3 tablespoons low-sodium soy sauce, divided
- 1 tablespoon peanut oil
- 3 tablespoons honey
- 3 tablespoons brown sugar
- 2 tablespoons ketchup
- ¼ cup pineapple juice

1. Select the BAKE function and preheat MAXX to 350ºF (177ºC).
2. Sprinkle the drumsticks with 1 tablespoon of lemon juice and 1 tablespoon of soy sauce. Place in the air fryer basket and drizzle with the peanut oil. Toss to coat. Bake for 18 minutes or until the chicken is almost done.
3. Meanwhile, in a metal bowl, combine the remaining 2 tablespoons of lemon juice, the remaining 2 tablespoons of soy sauce, honey, brown sugar, ketchup, and pineapple juice.
4. Add the cooked chicken to the bowl and stir to coat the chicken well with the sauce.
5. Place the metal bowl in the basket. Bake for 5 to 7 minutes or until the chicken is glazed and registers 165ºF (74ºC) on a meat thermometer. Serve warm.

Tempero Baiano Brazilian Chicken

Prep time: 5 minutes | Cook time: 20 minutes | Serves 4

- 1 teaspoon cumin seeds
- 1 teaspoon dried oregano
- 1 teaspoon dried parsley
- 1 teaspoon ground turmeric
- ½ teaspoon coriander seeds
- 1 teaspoon kosher salt
- ½ teaspoon black peppercorns
- ½ teaspoon cayenne pepper
- ¼ cup fresh lime juice
- 2 tablespoons olive oil
- 1½ pounds (680 g) chicken drumsticks

1. In a clean coffee grinder or spice mill, combine the cumin, oregano, parsley, turmeric, coriander seeds, salt, peppercorns, and cayenne. Process until finely ground.
2. In a small bowl, combine the ground spices with the lime juice and oil. Place the chicken in a resealable plastic bag. Add the marinade, seal, and massage until the chicken is well coated. Marinate at room temperature for 30 minutes or in the refrigerator for up to 24 hours.
3. Place the drumsticks skin-side up in the air fryer basket. Select the AIR FRY function and cook at 400ºF (204ºC) for 20 to 25 minutes, turning the drumsticks halfway through the cooking time. Use a meat thermometer to ensure that the chicken has reached an internal temperature of 165ºF (74ºC). Serve immediately.

Blackened Chicken Breasts

Prep time: 10 minutes | Cook time: 20 minutes | Serves 4

- 1 large egg, beaten
- ¾ cup Blackened seasoning
- 2 whole boneless, skinless chicken
- breasts (about 1 pound / 454 g each), halved
- Cooking spray

1. Line the air fryer basket with parchment paper.
2. Place the beaten egg in one shallow bowl and the Blackened seasoning in another shallow bowl.
3. One at a time, dip the chicken pieces in the beaten egg and the Blackened seasoning, coating thoroughly.
4. Place the chicken pieces on the parchment and spritz with cooking spray.
5. Select the AIR FRY function and cook at 360ºF (182ºC) for 10 minutes. Flip the chicken, spritz it with cooking spray, and air fry for 10 minutes more until the internal temperature reaches 165ºF (74ºC) and the chicken is no longer pink inside. Let sit for 5 minutes before serving.

Crisp Paprika Chicken Drumsticks

Prep time: 5 minutes | Cook time: 22 minutes | Serves 2

- 2 teaspoons paprika
- 1 teaspoon packed brown sugar
- 1 teaspoon garlic powder
- ½ teaspoon dry mustard
- ½ teaspoon salt
- Pinch pepper
- 4 (5-ounce / 142-g) chicken drumsticks, trimmed
- 1 teaspoon vegetable oil
- 1 scallion, green part only, sliced thin on bias

1. Combine paprika, sugar, garlic powder, mustard, salt, and pepper in a bowl. Pat drumsticks dry with paper towels. Using metal skewer, poke 10 to 15 holes in skin of each drumstick. Rub with oil and sprinkle evenly with spice mixture.
2. Arrange drumsticks in air fryer basket, spaced evenly apart, alternating ends. Select the AIR FRY function and cook at 400ºF (204ºC) for 22 to 25 minutes, or until chicken is crisp and registers 195ºF (91ºC), flipping chicken halfway through cooking.
3. Transfer chicken to serving platter, tent loosely with aluminum foil, and let rest for 5 minutes. Sprinkle with scallion and serve.

Air fryer oven Naked Chicken Tenders

Prep time: 5 minutes | Cook time: 7 minutes | Serves 4

Seasoning:
- 1 teaspoon kosher salt
- ½ teaspoon garlic powder
- ½ teaspoon onion powder
- ½ teaspoon chili powder
- ¼ teaspoon sweet paprika
- ¼ teaspoon freshly ground black pepper

Chicken:
- 8 chicken breast tenders (1 pound / 454 g total)
- 2 tablespoons mayonnaise

1. For the seasoning: In a small bowl, combine the salt, garlic powder, onion powder, chili powder, paprika, and pepper.
2. For the chicken: Place the chicken in a medium bowl and add the mayonnaise. Mix well to coat all over, then sprinkle with the seasoning mix.
3. Working in batches, arrange a single layer of the chicken in the air fryer basket. Select the AIR FRY function and cook at 375ºF (191ºC) for 6 to 7 minutes, flipping halfway, until cooked through in the center. Serve immediately.

Roasted Chicken Tenders with Veggies

Prep time: 10 minutes | Cook time: 18 to 20 minutes | Serves 4

- 1 pound (454 g) chicken tenders
- 1 tablespoon honey
- Pinch salt
- Freshly ground black pepper, to taste
- ½ cup soft fresh bread crumbs
- ½ teaspoon dried thyme
- 1 tablespoon olive oil
- 2 carrots, sliced
- 12 small red potatoes

1. Select the ROAST function and preheat MAXX to 380ºF (193ºC).
2. In a medium bowl, toss the chicken tenders with the honey, salt, and pepper.
3. In a shallow bowl, combine the bread crumbs, thyme, and olive oil, and mix.
4. Coat the tenders in the bread crumbs, pressing firmly onto the meat.
5. Place the carrots and potatoes in the air fryer basket and top with the chicken tenders.
6. Roast for 18 to 20 minutes or until the chicken is cooked to 165ºF (74ºC) and the vegetables are tender, shaking the basket halfway during the cooking time.
7. Serve warm.

Fried Buffalo Chicken Taquitos

Prep time: 15 minutes | Cook time: 5 to 10 minutes | Serves 6

- 8 ounces (227 g) fat-free cream cheese, softened
- ⅛ cup Buffalo sauce
- 2 cups shredded cooked chicken
- 12 (7-inch) low-carb flour tortillas
- Olive oil spray

1. Spray the air fryer basket lightly with olive oil spray.
2. In a large bowl, mix together the cream cheese and Buffalo sauce until well combined. Add the chicken and stir until combined.
3. Place the tortillas on a clean workspace. Spoon 2 to 3 tablespoons of the chicken mixture in a thin line down the center of each tortilla. Roll up the tortillas.
4. Place the tortillas in the air fryer basket, seam-side down. Spray each tortilla lightly with olive oil spray. You may need to cook the taquitos in batches.
5. Select the AIR FRY function and cook at 360ºF (182ºC) for 5 to 10 minutes, or until golden brown. Serve hot.

Piri-Piri Chicken Thighs

Prep time: 5 minutes | Cook time: 25 minutes | Serves 4

- ¼ cup piri-piri sauce
- 1 tablespoon freshly squeezed lemon juice
- 2 tablespoons brown sugar, divided
- 2 cloves garlic, minced
- 1 tablespoon extra-virgin olive oil
- 4 bone-in, skin-on chicken thighs, each weighing approximately 7 to 8 ounces (198 to 227 g)
- ½ teaspoon cornstarch

1. To make the marinade, whisk together the piri-piri sauce, lemon juice, 1 tablespoon of brown sugar, and the garlic in a small bowl. While whisking, slowly pour in the oil in a steady stream and continue to whisk until emulsified. Using a skewer, poke holes in the chicken thighs and place them in a small glass dish. Pour the marinade over the chicken and turn the thighs to coat them with the sauce. Cover the dish and refrigerate for at least 15 minutes and up to 1 hour.
2. Remove the chicken thighs from the dish, reserving the marinade, and place them skin-side down in the air fryer basket. Select the AIR FRY function and cook at 375ºF (191ºC) for 15 to 20 minutes, or until the internal temperature reaches 165ºF (74ºC).
3. Meanwhile, whisk the remaining brown sugar and the cornstarch into the marinade and microwave it on high power for 1 minute until it is bubbling and thickened to a glaze.
4. Once the chicken is cooked, turn the thighs over and brush them with the glaze. Air fry for a few additional minutes until the glaze browns and begins to char in spots.
5. Remove the chicken to a platter and serve with additional piri-piri sauce, if desired.

Israeli Chicken Schnitzel

Prep time: 5 minutes | Cook time: 10 minutes | Serves 4

- 2 large boneless, skinless chicken breasts, each weighing about 1 pound (454 g)
- 1 cup all-purpose flour
- 2 teaspoons garlic powder
- 2 teaspoons kosher salt
- 1 teaspoon black pepper
- 1 teaspoon paprika
- 2 eggs beaten with 2 tablespoons water
- 2 cups panko bread crumbs
- Vegetable oil spray
- Lemon juice, for serving

1. Place 1 chicken breast between 2 pieces of plastic wrap. Use a mallet or a rolling pin to pound the chicken until it is ¼ inch thick. Set aside. Repeat with the second breast. Whisk together the flour, garlic powder, salt, pepper, and paprika on a large plate. Place the panko in a separate shallow bowl or pie plate.
2. Dredge 1 chicken breast in the flour, shaking off any excess, then dip it in the egg mixture. Dredge the chicken breast in the panko, making sure to coat it completely. Shake off any excess panko. Place the battered chicken breast on a plate. Repeat with the second chicken breast.
3. Spray the air fryer basket with oil spray. Place 1 of the battered chicken breasts in the basket and spray the top with oil spray. Select the AIR FRY function and cook at 375ºF (191ºC) for 5 minutes, or until the top is browned. Flip the chicken and spray the second side with oil spray. Air fry until the second side is browned and crispy and the internal temperature reaches 165ºF (74ºC). Remove the first chicken breast from the air fryer oven and repeat with the second chicken breast.
4. Serve hot with lemon juice.

Dill Chicken Strips

Prep time: 15 minutes | Cook time: 10 minutes | Serves 4

- 2 whole boneless, skinless chicken breasts, halved lengthwise
- 1 cup Italian dressing
- 3 cups finely crushed potato chips
- 1 tablespoon dried dill weed
- 1 tablespoon garlic powder
- 1 large egg, beaten
- Cooking spray

1. In a large resealable bag, combine the chicken and Italian dressing. Seal the bag and refrigerate to marinate at least 1 hour.
2. In a shallow dish, stir together the potato chips, dill, and garlic powder. Place the beaten egg in a second shallow dish.
3. Remove the chicken from the marinade. Roll the chicken pieces in the egg and the potato chip mixture, coating thoroughly.
4. Select the BAKE function and preheat MAXX to 325ºF (163ºC). Line the air fryer basket with parchment paper.
5. Place the coated chicken on the parchment and spritz with cooking spray.
6. Bake for 5 minutes. Flip the chicken, spritz it with cooking spray, and bake for 5 minutes more until the outsides are crispy and the insides are no longer pink. Serve immediately.

Honey Rosemary Chicken

Prep time: 10 minutes | Cook time: 20 minutes | Serves 4

- ¼ cup balsamic vinegar
- ¼ cup honey
- 2 tablespoons olive oil
- 1 tablespoon dried rosemary leaves
- 1 teaspoon salt
- ½ teaspoon freshly ground black pepper
- 2 whole boneless, skinless chicken breasts (about 1 pound / 454 g each), halved
- Cooking spray

1. In a large resealable bag, combine the vinegar, honey, olive oil, rosemary, salt, and pepper. Add the chicken pieces, seal the bag, and refrigerate to marinate for at least 2 hours.
2. Select the BAKE function and preheat MAXX to 325ºF (163ºC). Line the air fryer basket with parchment paper.
3. Remove the chicken from the marinade and place it on the parchment. Spritz with cooking spray.
4. Bake for 10 minutes. Flip the chicken, spritz it with cooking spray, and bake for 10 minutes more until the internal temperature reaches 165ºF (74ºC) and the chicken is no longer pink inside. Let sit for 5 minutes before serving.

Mayonnaise-Mustard Chicken

Prep time: 10 minutes | Cook time: 15 minutes | Serves 4

- 6 tablespoons mayonnaise
- 2 tablespoons coarse-ground mustard
- 2 teaspoons honey (optional)
- 2 teaspoons curry powder
- 1 teaspoon kosher salt
- 1 teaspoon cayenne pepper
- 1 pound (454 g) chicken tenders

1. Select the BAKE function and preheat MAXX to 350ºF (177ºC).
2. In a large bowl, whisk together the mayonnaise, mustard, honey (if using), curry powder, salt, and cayenne. Transfer half of the mixture to a serving bowl to serve as a dipping sauce. Add the chicken tenders to the large bowl and toss until well coated.
3. Place the tenders in the air fryer basket and bake for 15 minutes. Use a meat thermometer to ensure the chicken has reached an internal temperature of 165ºF (74ºC).
4. Serve the chicken with the dipping sauce.

Chapter 5

Rotisserie Recipes

Rotisserie Chicken with Lemon

Prep time: 10 minutes | Cook time: 40 minutes | Serves 6

- 1 (4 pounds / 1.8 kg) whole chicken
- 2 teaspoons paprika
- 1½ teaspoons thyme
- 1 teaspoon onion powder
- 1 teaspoon garlic powder
- Salt and pepper, to taste
- ¼ cup butter, melted
- 2 tablespoons olive oil
- 1 lemon, sliced
- 2 sprigs rosemary

1. Remove the giblets from the chicken cavity and carefully loosen the skin starting at the neck.
2. In a bowl, mix together the paprika, thyme, onion powder, garlic powder, salt, and pepper. Set aside.
3. Rub the melted butter under the skin and pat the skin back into place.
4. Truss the chicken, ensuring the wings and legs are tied closely together and the cavity is closed up.
5. Drizzle the olive oil all over the chicken and rub it into the chicken.
6. Rub the spice mixture onto the chicken's skin.
7. Place the lemon slices and sprigs of rosemary into the cavity.
8. Using the rotisserie spit, push through the chicken and attach the rotisserie forks.
9. If desired, place aluminum foil onto the drip pan. (It makes for easier clean-up!)
10. Select the ROAST function and preheat MAXX to 380ºF (193ºC). Press ROTATE button and set time to 40 minutes.
11. Once the unit has preheated, place the prepared chicken with the rotisserie spit into the oven.
12. When cooking is complete, remove the chicken using the rotisserie handle and, using hot pads or gloves, carefully remove the chicken from the spit.
13. Let sit for 10 minutes before slicing and serving.

Greek Rotisserie Lamb Leg

Prep time: 25 minutes | Cook time: 1 hour 30 minutes | Serves 4 to 6

- 3 pounds (1.4 kg) leg of lamb, boned in

For the Marinade:

- 1 tablespoon lemon zest (about 1 lemon)
- 3 tablespoons lemon juice (about 1½ lemons)
- 3 cloves garlic, minced
- 1 teaspoon onion powder
- 1 teaspoon fresh thyme
- ¼ cup fresh oregano
- ¼ cup olive oil
- 1 teaspoon ground black pepper

For the Herb Dressing:

- 1 tablespoon lemon juice (about ½ lemon)
- ¼ cup chopped fresh oregano
- 1 teaspoon fresh thyme
- 1 tablespoon olive oil
- 1 teaspoon sea salt
- Ground black pepper, to taste

1. Place lamb leg into a large resealable plastic bag. Combine the ingredients for the marinade in a small bowl. Stir to mix well.
2. Pour the marinade over the lamb, making sure the meat is completely coated. Seal the bag and place in the refrigerator. Marinate for 4 to 6 hours before grilling.
3. Remove the lamb leg from the marinade. Using the rotisserie spit, push through the lamb leg and attach the rotisserie forks.
4. If desired, place aluminum foil onto the drip pan. (It makes for easier clean-up!)
5. Select the ROAST function and preheat MAXX to 350ºF (180ºC). Press ROTATE button and set time to 1 hour 30 minutes.
6. Once preheated, place the prepared lamb leg with rotisserie spit into the oven. Baste with marinade for every 30 minutes.
7. Meanwhile, combine the ingredients for the herb dressing in a bowl. Stir to mix well.
8. When cooking is complete, remove the lamb leg using the rotisserie handle and, using hot pads or gloves, carefully remove the lamb leg from the spit.
9. Cover lightly with aluminum foil for 8 to 10 minutes.
10. Carve the leg and arrange on a platter,. Drizzle with herb dressing. Serve immediately.

Easy Rotisserie Chicken

Prep time: 10 minutes | Cook time: 50 minutes | Serves 4

- 2 cups buttermilk
- ¼ cup olive oil
- 1 teaspoon garlic powder
- 1 tablespoon sea salt
- 1 whole chicken
- Salt and pepper, to taste

1. In a large bag, place the buttermilk, oil, garlic powder, and sea salt and mix to combine.
2. Add the whole chicken and let marinate for 24 hours up to two days.
3. Remove the chicken and sprinkle with the salt and pepper.
4. Truss the chicken, removing the wings and ensuring the legs are tied closely together and the thighs are held in place.
5. Using the rotisserie spit, push through the chicken and attach the rotisserie forks.
6. If desired, place aluminum foil onto the drip pan. (It makes for easier clean-up!)
7. Select the AIR FRY function and set the temperature to 380ºF (193ºC). Press ROTATE button and set time to 50 minutes.
8. Once the unit has preheated, place the prepared chicken with the rotisserie spit into the oven.
9. When cooking is complete, the chicken should be dark brown and internal temperature should measure 165 degrees (measure at the meatiest part of the thigh).
10. Remove the chicken using the rotisserie handle and, using hot pads or gloves, carefully remove the chicken from the spit.
11. Let sit for 10 minutes before slicing and serving.

Whole Rotisserie Chicken

Prep time: 10 minutes | Cook time: 45 minutes | Serves 4

- 3 pounds (1.4 kg) tied whole chicken
- 3 cloves garlic, halved
- 1 whole lemon, quartered
- 2 sprigs fresh rosemary whole
- 2 tablespoons olive oil

Chicken Rub:
- ½ teaspoon fresh ground pepper
- ½ teaspoon salt
- 1 teaspoon garlic powder
- 1 teaspoon dried oregano
- 1 teaspoon paprika
- 1 sprig rosemary (leaves only)

1. Mix together the rub ingredients in a small bowl. Set aside.

2. Place the chicken on a clean cutting board. Ensure the cavity of the chicken is clean. Stuff the chicken cavity with the garlic, lemon, and rosemary.
3. Tie your chicken with twine if needed. Pat the chicken dry.
4. Drizzle the olive oil all over and coat the entire chicken with a brush.
5. Shake the rub on the chicken and rub in until the chicken is covered.
6. Using the rotisserie spit, push through the chicken and attach the rotisserie forks.
7. If desired, place aluminum foil onto the drip pan. (It makes for easier clean-up!)
8. Select the AIR FRY function and set the temperature to 375ºF (190ºC). Press ROTATE button and set time to 40 minutes.
9. Once the unit has preheated, place the prepared chicken with the rotisserie spit into the oven.
10. At 40 minutes, check the temperature every 5 minutes until the chicken reaches 165ºF (74ºC) in the breast, or 165ºF (85ºC) in the thigh.
11. Once cooking is complete, remove the chicken using the rotisserie handle and, using hot pads or gloves, carefully remove the chicken from the spit.
12. Let the chicken sit, covered, for 5 to 10 minutes.
13. Slice and serve.

Air Fried Beef Roast

Prep time: 5 minutes | Cook time: 38 minutes | Serves 6

- 2.5 pound (1.1 kg) beef roast
- 1 tablespoon olive oil
- 1 tablespoon Poultry seasoning

1. Tie the beef roast and rub the olive oil all over the roast. Sprinkle with the seasoning.
2. Using the rotisserie spit, push through the beef roast and attach the rotisserie forks.
3. If desired, place aluminum foil onto the drip pan. (It makes for easier clean-up!)
4. Select the AIR FRY function and set the temperature to 360ºF (182ºC). Press ROTATE button and set time to 38 minutes for medium rare beef.
5. Place the prepared chicken with rotisserie spit into the oven.
6. When cooking is complete, remove the beef roast using the rotisserie handle and, using hot pads or gloves, carefully remove the beef roast from the spit.
7. Let cool for 5 minutes before serving.

Chapter 6

Meats

Pepperoni and Bell Pepper Pockets

Prep time: 5 minutes | Cook time: 8 minutes | Serves 4

- 4 bread slices, 1-inch thick
- Olive oil, for misting
- 24 slices pepperoni
- 1 ounce (28 g) roasted red

  peppers, drained and patted dry
- 1 ounce (28 g) Pepper Jack cheese, cut into 4 slices

1. Spray both sides of bread slices with olive oil.
2. Stand slices upright and cut a deep slit in the top to create a pocket (almost to the bottom crust, but not all the way through).
3. Stuff each bread pocket with 6 slices of pepperoni, a large strip of roasted red pepper, and a slice of cheese.
4. Put bread pockets in air fryer basket, standing up. Select the AIR FRY function and cook at 360ºF (182ºC) for 8 minutes, until filling is heated through and bread is lightly browned.
5. Serve hot.

Char Siew

Prep time: 10 minutes | Cook time: 20 minutes | Serves 4 to 6

- 1 strip of pork shoulder butt with a good amount of fat marbling
- Olive oil, for brushing the pan

Marinade:
- 1 teaspoon sesame oil
- 4 tablespoons raw honey
- 1 teaspoon low-sodium dark soy sauce
- 1 teaspoon light soy sauce
- 1 tablespoon rose wine
- 2 tablespoons Hoisin sauce

1. Combine all the marinade ingredients together in a Ziploc bag. Put pork in bag, making sure all sections of pork strip are engulfed in the marinade. Chill for 3 to 24 hours.
2. Take out the strip 30 minutes before planning to roast.
3. Select the ROAST function and preheat MAXX to 350ºF (177ºC).
4. Put foil on small pan and brush with olive oil. Put marinated pork strip onto prepared pan.
5. Roast in the preheated air fryer oven for 20 minutes.
6. Glaze with marinade every 5 to 10 minutes.
7. Remove strip and leave to cool a few minutes before slicing.
8. Serve immediately.

Miso Marinated Steak

Prep time: 5 minutes | Cook time: 12 minutes | Serves 4

- ¾ pound (340 g) flank steak
- 1½ tablespoons sake
- 1 tablespoon brown miso paste
- 1 teaspoon honey
- 2 cloves garlic, pressed
- 1 tablespoon olive oil

1. Put all the ingredients in a Ziploc bag. Shake to cover the steak well with the seasonings and refrigerate for at least 1 hour.
2. Coat all sides of the steak with cooking spray. Put the steak in the baking pan.
3. Select the AIR FRY function and cook at 400ºF (204ºC) for 12 minutes, turning the steak twice during the cooking time, then serve immediately.

Orange Pork Tenderloin

Prep time: 15 minutes | Cook time: 23 minutes | Serves 3 to 4

- 2 tablespoons brown sugar
- 2 teaspoons cornstarch
- 2 teaspoons Dijon mustard
- ½ cup orange juice
- ½ teaspoon soy sauce
- 2 teaspoons grated fresh ginger
- ¼ cup white wine
- Zest of 1 orange
- 1 pound (454 g) pork tenderloin
- Salt and freshly ground black pepper, to taste
- Oranges, halved, for garnish
- Fresh parsley, for garnish

1. Combine the brown sugar, cornstarch, Dijon mustard, orange juice, soy sauce, ginger, white wine and orange zest in a small saucepan and bring the mixture to a boil on the stovetop. Lower the heat and simmer while you air fry the pork tenderloin or until the sauce has thickened.
2. Season all sides of the pork tenderloin with salt and freshly ground black pepper. Transfer the tenderloin to the air fryer basket.
3. Select the AIR FRY function and cook at 370ºF (188ºC) for 20 to 23 minutes, or until the internal temperature reaches 145ºF (63ºC). Flip the tenderloin over halfway through the cooking process and baste with the sauce.
4. Transfer the tenderloin to a cutting board and let it rest for 5 minutes. Slice the pork at a slight angle and serve immediately with orange halves and fresh parsley.

Mushroom and Beef Meatloaf

Prep time: 10 minutes | Cook time: 25 minutes | Serves 4

- 1 pound (454 g) ground beef
- 1 egg, beaten
- 1 mushrooms, sliced
- 1 tablespoon thyme
- 1 small onion, chopped
- 3 tablespoons bread crumbs
- Ground black pepper, to taste

1. Select the BAKE function and preheat MAXX to 400ºF (204ºC).
2. Put all the ingredients into a large bowl and combine entirely.
3. Transfer the meatloaf mixture into the loaf pan and move it to the air fryer basket.
4. Bake for 25 minutes. Slice up before serving.

Sumptuous Pizza Tortilla Rolls

Prep time: 10 minutes | Cook time: 6 minutes | Serves 4

- 1 teaspoon butter
- ½ medium onion, slivered
- ½ red or green bell pepper, julienned
- 4 ounces (113 g) fresh white mushrooms, chopped
- ½ cup pizza sauce
- 8 flour tortillas
- 8 thin slices deli ham
- 24 pepperoni slices
- 1 cup shredded Mozzarella cheese
- Cooking spray

1. Select the BAKE function and preheat MAXX to 390ºF (199ºC).
2. Put butter, onions, bell pepper, and mushrooms in a baking pan. Bake in the preheated air fryer oven for 3 minutes. Stir and cook 3 to 4 minutes longer until just crisp and tender. Remove pan and set aside.
3. To assemble rolls, spread about 2 teaspoons of pizza sauce on one half of each tortilla. Top with a slice of ham and 3 slices of pepperoni. Divide sautéed vegetables among tortillas and top with cheese.
4. Roll up tortillas, secure with toothpicks if needed, and spray with oil.
5. Put 4 rolls in air fryer basket. Switch from BAKE to AIR FRY and air fry for 4 minutes. Turn and air fry for 4 minutes, until heated through and lightly browned.
6. Repeat with the remaining pizza rolls.
7. Serve immediately.

Barbecue Pork Ribs

Prep time: 5 minutes | Cook time: 30 minutes | Serves 4

- 1 tablespoon barbecue dry rub
- 1 teaspoon mustard
- 1 tablespoon apple cider vinegar
- 1 teaspoon sesame oil
- 1 pound (454 g) pork ribs, chopped

1. Combine the dry rub, mustard, apple cider vinegar, and sesame oil, then coat the ribs with this mixture. Refrigerate the ribs for 20 minutes.
2. When the ribs are ready, place them in the air fryer oven. Select the AIR FRY function and cook at 360ºF (182ºC) for 15 minutes. Flip them and air fry on the other side for a further 15 minutes.
3. Serve immediately.

Lollipop Lamb Chops

Prep time: 15 minutes | Cook time: 7 minutes | Serves 4

- ½ small clove garlic
- ¼ cup packed fresh parsley
- ¾ cup packed fresh mint
- ½ teaspoon lemon juice
- ¼ cup grated Parmesan cheese
- $1/3$ cup shelled pistachios
- ¼ teaspoon salt
- ½ cup olive oil
- 8 lamb chops (1 rack)
- 2 tablespoons vegetable oil
- Salt and freshly ground black pepper, to taste
- 1 tablespoon dried rosemary, chopped
- 1 tablespoon dried thyme

1. Make the pesto by combining the garlic, parsley and mint in a food processor and process until finely chopped. Add the lemon juice, Parmesan cheese, pistachios and salt. Process until all the ingredients have turned into a paste. With the processor running, slowly pour the olive oil in. Scrape the sides of the processor with a spatula and process for another 30 seconds.
2. Rub both sides of the lamb chops with vegetable oil and season with salt, pepper, rosemary and thyme, pressing the herbs into the meat gently with the fingers. Transfer the lamb chops to the air fryer basket.
3. Select the AIR FRY function and cook at 400ºF (204ºC) for 5 minutes. Flip the chops over and air fry for an additional 2 minutes.
4. Serve the lamb chops with mint pesto drizzled on top.

Potato and Prosciutto Salad

Prep time: 10 minutes | Cook time: 7 minutes | Serves 8

Salad:
- 4 pounds (1.8 kg) potatoes, boiled and cubed
- 15 slices prosciutto, diced
- 2 cups shredded Cheddar cheese

Dressing:
- 15 ounces (425 g) sour cream
- 2 tablespoons mayonnaise
- 1 teaspoon salt
- 1 teaspoon black pepper
- 1 teaspoon dried basil

1. Put the potatoes, prosciutto, and Cheddar in a baking dish. Put it in the air fryer oven.
2. Select the AIR FRY function and cook at 350ºF (177ºC) for 7 minutes.
3. In a separate bowl, mix the sour cream, mayonnaise, salt, pepper, and basil using a whisk.
4. Coat the salad with the dressing and serve.

Citrus Pork Loin Roast

Prep time: 10 minutes | Cook time: 45 minutes | Serves 8

- 1 tablespoon lime juice
- 1 tablespoon orange marmalade
- 1 teaspoon coarse brown mustard
- 1 teaspoon curry powder
- 1 teaspoon dried lemongrass
- 2 pound (907 g) boneless pork loin roast
- Salt and ground black pepper, to taste
- Cooking spray

1. Mix the lime juice, marmalade, mustard, curry powder, and lemongrass.
2. Rub mixture all over the surface of the pork loin. Season with salt and pepper.
3. Spray air fryer basket with cooking spray and place pork roast diagonally in the basket.
4. Select the AIR FRY function and cook at 360ºF (182ºC) for 45 minutes, until the internal temperature reaches at least 145ºF (63ºC).
5. Wrap roast in foil and let rest for 10 minutes before slicing.
6. Serve immediately.

Pork and Pinto Bean Gorditas

Prep time: 20 minutes | Cook time: 21 minutes | Serves 4

- 1 pound (454 g) lean ground pork
- 2 tablespoons chili powder
- 2 tablespoons ground cumin
- 1 teaspoon dried oregano
- 2 teaspoons paprika
- 1 teaspoon garlic powder
- ½ cup water
- 1 (15-ounce / 425-g) can pinto beans, drained and rinsed
- ½ cup taco sauce
- Salt and freshly ground black
- pepper, to taste
- 2 cups grated Cheddar cheese
- 5 (12-inch) flour tortillas
- 4 (8-inch) crispy corn tortilla shells
- 4 cups shredded lettuce
- 1 tomato, diced
- ⅓ cup sliced black olives
- Sour cream, for serving
- Tomato salsa, for serving
- Cooking spray

1. Spritz the air fryer basket with cooking spray.
2. Put the ground pork in the air fryer basket. Select the AIR FRY function and cook at 400ºF (204ºC) for 10 minutes, stirring a few times to gently break up the meat. Combine the chili powder, cumin, oregano, paprika, garlic powder and water in a small bowl. Stir the spice mixture into the browned pork. Stir in the beans and taco sauce and air fry for an additional minute. Transfer the pork mixture to a bowl. Season with salt and freshly ground black pepper.
3. Sprinkle ½ cup of the grated cheese in the center of the flour tortillas, leaving a 2-inch border around the edge free of cheese and filling. Divide the pork mixture among the four tortillas, placing it on top of the cheese. Put a crunchy corn tortilla on top of the pork and top with shredded lettuce, diced tomatoes, and black olives. Cut the remaining flour tortilla into 4 quarters. These quarters of tortilla will serve as the bottom of the gordita. Put one quarter tortilla on top of each gordita and fold the edges of the bottom flour tortilla up over the sides, enclosing the filling. While holding the seams down, brush the bottom of the gordita with olive oil and place the seam side down on the countertop while you finish the remaining three gorditas.
4. Adjust the temperature to 380ºF (193ºC).
5. Air fry one gordita at a time. Transfer the gordita carefully to the air fryer basket, seam side down. Brush or spray the top tortilla with oil and air fry for 5 minutes. Carefully turn the gordita over and air fry for an additional 4 to 5 minutes until both sides are browned. When finished air frying all four gorditas, layer them back into the air fryer oven for an additional minute to make sure they are all warm before serving with sour cream and salsa.

Air Fried Lamb Ribs

Prep time: 5 minutes | Cook time: 18 minutes | Serves 4

- 2 tablespoons mustard
- 1 pound (454 g) lamb ribs
- 1 teaspoon rosemary, chopped
- Salt and ground black pepper, to
- taste
- ¼ cup mint leaves, chopped
- 1 cup Greek yogurt

1. Use a brush to apply the mustard to the lamb ribs, and season with rosemary, salt, and pepper. Transfer to the air fryer basket.
2. Select the AIR FRY function and cook at 350ºF (177ºC) for 18 minutes.
3. Meanwhile, combine the mint leaves and yogurt in a bowl.
4. Remove the lamb ribs from the air fryer oven when cooked and serve with the mint yogurt.

Chapter 7

Wraps and Sandwiches

Veggie Pita Sandwich

Prep time: 10 minutes | Cook time: 9 to 12 minutes | Serves 4

- 1 baby eggplant, peeled and chopped
- 1 red bell pepper, sliced
- ½ cup diced red onion
- ½ cup shredded carrot
- 1 teaspoon olive oil
- ⅓ cup low-fat Greek yogurt
- ½ teaspoon dried tarragon
- 2 low-sodium whole-wheat pita breads, halved crosswise

1. Select the ROAST function and preheat MAXX to 390ºF (199ºC).
2. In a baking pan, stir together the eggplant, red bell pepper, red onion, carrot, and olive oil. Put the vegetable mixture into the air fryer basket and roast for 7 to 9 minutes, stirring once, until the vegetables are tender. Drain if necessary.
3. In a small bowl, thoroughly mix the yogurt and tarragon until well combined.
4. Stir the yogurt mixture into the vegetables. Stuff one-fourth of this mixture into each pita pocket.
5. Place the sandwiches in the air fryer oven. Switch from ROAST to BAKE and bake for 2 to 3 minutes, or until the bread is toasted.
6. Serve immediately.

Bacon and Bell Pepper Sandwich

Prep time: 10 minutes | Cook time: 6 minutes | Serves 4

- ⅓ cup spicy barbecue sauce
- 2 tablespoons honey
- 8 slices cooked bacon, cut into thirds
- 1 red bell pepper, sliced
- 1 yellow bell pepper, sliced
- 3 pita pockets, cut in half
- 1¼ cups torn butter lettuce leaves
- 2 tomatoes, sliced

1. Select the ROAST function and preheat MAXX to 350ºF (177ºC).
2. In a small bowl, combine the barbecue sauce and the honey. Brush this mixture lightly onto the bacon slices and the red and yellow pepper slices.
3. Put the peppers into the air fryer basket and roast for 4 minutes. Then shake the basket, add the bacon, and roast for 2 minutes or until the bacon is browned and the peppers are tender.
4. Fill the pita halves with the bacon, peppers, any remaining barbecue sauce, lettuce, and tomatoes, and serve immediately.

Chicken Pita Sandwich

Prep time: 10 minutes | Cook time: 9 to 11 minutes | Serves 4

- 2 boneless, skinless chicken breasts, cut into 1-inch cubes
- 1 small red onion, sliced
- 1 red bell pepper, sliced
- 1/3 cup Italian salad dressing,
- divided
- 1/2 teaspoon dried thyme
- 4 pita pockets, split
- 2 cups torn butter lettuce
- 1 cup chopped cherry tomatoes

1. Select the BAKE function and preheat MAXX to 380ºF (193ºC).
2. Place the chicken, onion, and bell pepper in the air fryer basket. Drizzle with 1 tablespoon of the Italian salad dressing, add the thyme, and toss.
3. Bake for 9 to 11 minutes, or until the chicken is 165ºF (74ºC) on a food thermometer, stirring once during cooking time.
4. Transfer the chicken and vegetables to a bowl and toss with the remaining salad dressing.
5. Assemble sandwiches with the pita pockets, butter lettuce, and cherry tomatoes. Serve immediately.

Tuna Muffin Sandwich

Prep time: 8 minutes | Cook time: 4 to 8 minutes | Serves 4

- 1 (6-ounce / 170-g) can chunk light tuna, drained
- 1/4 cup mayonnaise
- 2 tablespoons mustard
- 1 tablespoon lemon juice
- 2 green onions, minced
- 3 English muffins, split with a fork
- 3 tablespoons softened butter
- 6 thin slices Provolone or Muenster cheese

1. Select the BAKE function and preheat MAXX to 390ºF (199ºC).
2. In a small bowl, combine the tuna, mayonnaise, mustard, lemon juice, and green onions. Set aside.
3. Butter the cut side of the English muffins. Bake, butter-side up, in the air fryer oven for 2 to 4 minutes, or until light golden brown. Remove the muffins from the air fryer basket.
4. Top each muffin with one slice of cheese and return to the air fryer oven. Bake for 2 to 4 minutes or until the cheese melts and starts to brown.
5. Remove the muffins from the air fryer oven, top with the tuna mixture, and serve.

Classic Sloppy Joes

Prep time: 10 minutes | Cook time: 17 to 19 minutes | Makes 4 large sandwiches or 8 sliders

- 1 pound (454 g) very lean ground beef
- 1 teaspoon onion powder
- 1/3 cup ketchup
- 1/4 cup water
- 1/2 teaspoon celery seed
- 1 tablespoon lemon juice
- 1 1/2 teaspoons brown sugar
- 1 1/4 teaspoons low-sodium Worcestershire sauce
- 1/2 teaspoon salt (optional)
- 1/2 teaspoon vinegar
- 1/8 teaspoon dry mustard
- Hamburger or slider buns, for serving
- Cooking spray

1. Select the ROAST function and preheat MAXX to 390ºF (199ºC). Spray the air fryer basket with cooking spray.
2. Break raw ground beef into small chunks and pile into the basket. Roast for 5 minutes. Stir to break apart and roast for 3 minutes. Stir and roast for 2 to 4 minutes longer, or until meat is well done.
3. Remove the meat from the air fryer oven, drain, and use a knife and fork to crumble into small pieces.
4. Give your air fryer basket a quick rinse to remove any bits of meat.
5. Place all the remaining ingredients, except for the buns, in a baking pan and mix together. Add the meat and stir well.
6. Switch from ROAST to BAKE. Bake at 330ºF (166ºC) for 5 minutes. Stir and bake for 2 minutes.
7. Scoop onto buns. Serve hot.

Smoky Chicken Sandwich

Prep time: 10 minutes | Cook time: 11 minutes | Serves 2

- 2 boneless, skinless chicken breasts (8 ounces / 227 g each), sliced horizontally in half and separated into 4 thinner cutlets
- Kosher salt and freshly ground black pepper, to taste
- 1/2 cup all-purpose flour
- 3 large eggs, lightly beaten
- 1/2 cup dried bread crumbs
- 1 tablespoon smoked paprika
- Cooking spray
- 1/2 cup marinara sauce
- 6 ounces (170 g) smoked Mozzarella cheese, grated
- 2 store-bought soft, sesame-seed hamburger or Italian buns, split

1. Season the chicken cutlets all over with salt and pepper. Set up three shallow bowls: Place the flour in the first bowl, the eggs in the second, and stir together the bread crumbs and smoked paprika in the third. Coat the chicken pieces in the flour, then dip fully in the egg. Dredge in the paprika bread crumbs, then transfer to a wire rack set over a baking sheet and spray both sides liberally with cooking spray.
2. Transfer 2 of the chicken cutlets to the air fryer oven. Select the AIR FRY function and cook at 350ºF (177ºC) for 6 minutes, or until beginning to brown. Spread each cutlet with 2 tablespoons of the marinara sauce and sprinkle with one-quarter of the smoked Mozzarella.
3. Increase the temperature to 400ºF (204ºC) and air fry for 5 minutes more, or until the chicken is cooked through and crisp and the cheese is melted and golden brown.
4. Transfer the cutlets to a plate, stack on top of each other, and place inside a bun. Repeat with the remaining chicken cutlets, marinara, smoked Mozzarella, and bun.
5. Serve the sandwiches warm.

Cheesy Shrimp Sandwich

Prep time: 10 minutes | Cook time: 5 to 7 minutes | Serves 4

- 1¼ cups shredded Colby, Cheddar, or Havarti cheese
- 1 (6-ounce / 170-g) can tiny shrimp, drained
- 3 tablespoons mayonnaise
- 2 tablespoons minced green onion
- 4 slices whole grain or whole-wheat bread
- 2 tablespoons softened butter

1. In a medium bowl, combine the cheese, shrimp, mayonnaise, and green onion, and mix well.
2. Spread this mixture on two of the slices of bread. Top with the other slices of bread to make two sandwiches. Spread the sandwiches lightly with butter.
3. Select the AIR FRY function and cook at 400ºF (204ºC) for 5 to 7 minutes, or until the bread is browned and crisp and the cheese is melted.
4. Cut in half and serve warm.

Chapter 8

Appetizers and Snacks

Artichoke-Spinach Dip

Prep time: 10 minutes | Cook time: 10 minutes | Makes 3 cups

- 1 (14-ounce / 397-g) can artichoke hearts packed in water, drained and chopped
- 1 (10-ounce / 284-g) package frozen spinach, thawed and drained
- 1 teaspoon minced garlic
- 2 tablespoons mayonnaise
- ¼ cup nonfat plain Greek yogurt
- ¼ cup shredded part-skim Mozzarella cheese
- ¼ cup grated Parmesan cheese
- ¼ teaspoon freshly ground black pepper
- Cooking spray

1. Wrap the artichoke hearts and spinach in a paper towel and squeeze out any excess liquid, then transfer the vegetables to a large bowl.
2. Add the minced garlic, mayonnaise, plain Greek yogurt, Mozzarella, Parmesan, and black pepper to the large bowl, stirring well to combine.
3. Spray a baking pan with cooking spray, then transfer the dip mixture to the pan. Select the AIR FRY function and cook at 360ºF (182ºC) for 10 minutes.
4. Remove the dip from the air fryer oven and allow to cool in the pan on a wire rack for 10 minutes before serving.

Rosemary Baked Cashews

Prep time: 5 minutes | Cook time: 3 minutes | Makes 2 cups

- 2 sprigs of fresh rosemary (1 chopped and 1 whole)
- 1 teaspoon olive oil
- 1 teaspoon kosher salt
- ½ teaspoon honey
- 2 cups roasted and unsalted whole cashews
- Cooking spray

1. Select the BAKE function and preheat MAXX to 300ºF (149ºC).
2. In a medium bowl, whisk together the chopped rosemary, olive oil, kosher salt, and honey. Set aside.
3. Spray the air fryer basket with cooking spray, then place the cashews and the whole rosemary sprig in the basket and bake for 3 minutes.
4. Remove the cashews and rosemary from the air fryer oven, then discard the rosemary and add the cashews to the olive oil mixture, tossing to coat.
5. Allow to cool for 15 minutes before serving.

Spicy Chicken Bites

Prep time: 10 minutes | Cook time: 10 to 12 minutes | Makes 30 bites

- 8 ounces boneless and skinless chicken thighs, cut into 30 pieces
- ¼ teaspoon kosher salt
- 2 tablespoons hot sauce
- Cooking spray

1. Spray the air fryer basket with cooking spray and season the chicken bites with the kosher salt, then place in the basket.
2. Select the AIR FRY function and cook at 390ºF (199ºC) for 10 to 12 minutes, or until crispy.
3. While the chicken bites cook, pour the hot sauce into a large bowl.
4. Remove the bites and add to the sauce bowl, tossing to coat.
5. Serve warm.

Crispy Cajun Dill Pickle Chips

Prep time: 5 minutes | Cook time: 10 minutes | Makes 16 slices

- ¼ cup all-purpose flour
- ½ cup panko bread crumbs
- 1 large egg, beaten
- 2 teaspoons Cajun seasoning
- 2 large dill pickles, sliced into 8 rounds each
- Cooking spray

1. Place the all-purpose flour, panko bread crumbs, and egg into 3 separate shallow bowls, then stir the Cajun seasoning into the flour.
2. Dredge each pickle chip in the flour mixture, then the egg, and finally the bread crumbs. Shake off any excess, then place each coated pickle chip on a plate.
3. Spritz the air fryer basket with cooking spray, then place 8 pickle chips in the basket. Select the AIR FRY function and cook at 390ºF (199ºC) for 5 minutes, or until crispy and golden brown. Repeat this process with the remaining pickle chips.
4. Remove the chips and allow to slightly cool on a wire rack before serving.

Spinach and Crab Meat Cups

Prep time: 10 minutes | Cook time: 10 minutes | Makes 30 cups

- 1 (6-ounce / 170-g) can crab meat, drained to yield $1/_3$ cup meat
- ¼ cup frozen spinach, thawed, drained, and chopped
- 1 clove garlic, minced
- ½ cup grated Parmesan cheese
- 3 tablespoons plain yogurt
- ¼ teaspoon lemon juice
- ½ teaspoon Worcestershire sauce
- 30 mini frozen phyllo shells, thawed
- Cooking spray

1. Remove any bits of shell that might remain in the crab meat.
2. Mix the crab meat, spinach, garlic, and cheese together.
3. Stir in the yogurt, lemon juice, and Worcestershire sauce and mix well.
4. Spoon a teaspoon of filling into each phyllo shell.
5. Spray the air fryer basket with cooking spray and arrange half the shells in the basket.
6. Select the AIR FRY function and cook at 390ºF (199ºC) for 5 minutes. Repeat with the remaining shells.
7. Serve immediately.

Bacon-Wrapped Dates

Prep time: 10 minutes | Cook time: 10 to 14 minutes | Serves 6

- 12 dates, pitted
- 6 slices high-quality bacon, cut in
- half
- Cooking spray

1. Select the BAKE function and preheat MAXX to 360ºF (182ºC).
2. Wrap each date with half a bacon slice and secure with a toothpick.
3. Spray the air fryer basket with cooking spray, then place 6 bacon-wrapped dates in the basket and bake for 5 to 7 minutes or until the bacon is crispy. Repeat this process with the remaining dates.
4. Remove the dates and allow to cool on a wire rack for 5 minutes before serving.

Cajun Zucchini Chips

Prep time: 5 minutes | Cook time: 15 to 16 minutes | Serves 4

- 2 large zucchini, cut into ⅛-inch-thick slices
- 2 teaspoons Cajun seasoning
- Cooking spray

1. Spray the air fryer basket lightly with cooking spray.
2. Put the zucchini slices in a medium bowl and spray them generously with cooking spray.
3. Sprinkle the Cajun seasoning over the zucchini and stir to make sure they are evenly coated with oil and seasoning.
4. Place the slices in a single layer in the air fryer basket, making sure not to overcrowd. You will need to cook these in several batches.
5. Select the AIR FRY function and cook at 370ºF (188ºC) for 8 minutes. Flip the slices over and air fry for an additional 7 to 8 minutes, or until they are as crisp and brown as you prefer.
6. Serve immediately.

Honey Sriracha Chicken Wings

Prep time: 5 minutes | Cook time: 30 minutes | Serves 4

- 1 tablespoon Sriracha hot sauce
- 1 tablespoon honey
- 1 garlic clove, minced
- ½ teaspoon kosher salt
- 16 chicken wings and drumettes
- Cooking spray

1. In a large bowl, whisk together the Sriracha hot sauce, honey, minced garlic, and kosher salt, then add the chicken and toss to coat.
2. Spray the air fryer basket with cooking spray, then place 8 wings in the basket.
3. Select the AIR FRY function and cook at 360ºF (182ºC) for 15 minutes, turning halfway through. Repeat with the remaining wings.
4. Remove the wings and allow to cool on a wire rack for 10 minutes before serving.

Chapter 9

Desserts

Chocolate Coconut Brownies

Prep time: 15 minutes | Cook time: 15 minutes | Serves 8

- ½ cup coconut oil
- 2 ounces (57 g) dark chocolate
- 1 cup sugar
- 2½ tablespoons water
- 4 whisked eggs
- ¼ teaspoon ground cinnamon
- ½ teaspoons ground anise star
- ¼ teaspoon coconut extract
- ½ teaspoons vanilla extract
- 1 tablespoon honey
- ½ cup flour
- ½ cup desiccated coconut
- Sugar, for dusting

1. Select the BAKE function and preheat MAXX to 355ºF (179ºC).
2. Melt the coconut oil and dark chocolate in the microwave.
3. Combine with the sugar, water, eggs, cinnamon, anise, coconut extract, vanilla, and honey in a large bowl.
4. Stir in the flour and desiccated coconut. Incorporate everything well.
5. Lightly grease a baking dish with butter. Transfer the mixture to the dish.
6. Put the dish in the air fryer oven and bake for 15 minutes.
7. Remove from the air fryer oven and allow to cool slightly.
8. Take care when taking it out of the baking dish. Slice it into squares.
9. Dust with sugar before serving.

Simple Pineapple Sticks

Prep time: 5 minutes | Cook time: 10 minutes | Serves 4

- ½ fresh pineapple, cut into sticks
- ¼ cup desiccated coconut

1. Coat the pineapple sticks in the desiccated coconut and put each one in the air fryer basket.
2. Select the AIR FRY function and cook at 400ºF (204ºC) for 10 minutes.
3. Serve immediately

Chocolate S'mores

Prep time: 5 minutes | Cook time: 3 minutes | Serves 12

- 12 whole cinnamon graham crackers
- 2 (1.55-ounce / 44-g) chocolate
- bars, broken into 12 pieces
- 12 marshmallows

1. Select the BAKE function and preheat MAXX to 350ºF (177ºC).
2. Halve each graham cracker into 2 squares.
3. Put 6 graham cracker squares in the air fryer oven. Do not stack. Put a piece of chocolate into each. Bake for 2 minutes.
4. Open the air fryer oven and add a marshmallow onto each piece of melted chocolate. Bake for 1 additional minute.
5. Remove the cooked s'mores from the air fryer oven, then repeat with the remaining 6 s'mores.
6. Top with the remaining graham cracker squares and serve.

Easy Chocolate Donuts

Prep time: 5 minutes | Cook time: 8 minutes | Serves 8

- 1 (8-ounce / 227-g) can jumbo biscuits
- Cooking oil
- Chocolate sauce, for drizzling

1. Separate the biscuit dough into 8 biscuits and place them on a flat work surface. Use a small circle cookie cutter or a biscuit cutter to cut a hole in the center of each biscuit. You can also cut the holes using a knife.
2. Spray the air fryer basket with cooking oil.
3. Put 4 donuts in the air fryer oven. Do not stack. Spray with cooking oil.
4. Select the AIR FRY function and cook at 375ºF (191ºC) for 4 minutes.
5. Open the air fryer oven and flip the donuts. Air fry for an additional 4 minutes.
6. Remove the cooked donuts from the air fryer oven. Repeat with the remaining 4 donuts.
7. Drizzle chocolate sauce over the donuts and enjoy while warm.

Cinnamon and Pecan Pie

Prep time: 10 minutes | Cook time: 25 minutes | Serves 4

- 1 pie dough
- ½ teaspoons cinnamon
- ¾ teaspoon vanilla extract
- 2 eggs
- ¾ cup maple syrup
- ⅛ teaspoon nutmeg
- 3 tablespoons melted butter, divided
- 2 tablespoons sugar
- ½ cup chopped pecans

1. In a small bowl, coat the pecans in 1 tablespoon of melted butter.
2. Transfer the pecans to the air fryer oven. Select the AIR FRY function and cook at 370ºF (188ºC) for 10 minutes.
3. Put the pie dough in a greased pie pan and add the pecans on top.
4. In a bowl, mix the rest of the ingredients. Pour this over the pecans.
5. Put the pan in the air fryer oven. Switch from AIR FRY to BAKE and bake for 25 minutes.
6. Serve immediately.

Pineapple and Chocolate Cake

Prep time: 10 minutes | Cook time: 35 to 40 minutes | Serves 4

- 2 cups flour
- 4 ounces (113 g) butter, melted
- ¼ cup sugar
- ½ pound (227 g) pineapple, chopped
- ½ cup pineapple juice
- 1 ounce (28 g) dark chocolate, grated
- 1 large egg
- 2 tablespoons skimmed milk

1. Select the BAKE function and preheat MAXX to 370ºF (188ºC).
2. Grease a cake tin with a little oil or butter.
3. In a bowl, combine the butter and flour to create a crumbly consistency.
4. Add the sugar, chopped pineapple, juice, and grated dark chocolate and mix well.
5. In a separate bowl, combine the egg and milk. Add this mixture to the flour mixture and stir well until a soft dough forms.
6. Pour the mixture into the cake tin and transfer to the air fryer oven.
7. Bake for 35 to 40 minutes.
8. Serve immediately.

Chocolate Molten Cake

Prep time: 5 minutes | Cook time: 10 minutes | Serves 4

- 3.5 ounces (99 g) butter, melted
- 3½ tablespoons sugar
- 3.5 ounces (99 g) chocolate,
- melted
- 1½ tablespoons flour
- 2 eggs

1. Select the BAKE function and preheat MAXX to 375ºF (191ºC).
2. Grease four ramekins with a little butter.
3. Rigorously combine the eggs, butter, and sugar before stirring in the melted chocolate.
4. Slowly fold in the flour.
5. Spoon an equal amount of the mixture into each ramekin.
6. Put them in the air fryer oven and bake for 10 minutes
7. Put the ramekins upside-down on plates and let the cakes fall out. Serve hot.

Banana and Walnut Cake

Prep time: 10 minutes | Cook time: 25 minutes | Serves 6

- 1 pound (454 g) bananas, mashed
- 8 ounces (227 g) flour
- 6 ounces (170 g) sugar
- 3.5 ounces (99 g) walnuts,
- chopped
- 2.5 ounces (71 g) butter, melted
- 2 eggs, lightly beaten
- ¼ teaspoon baking soda

1. Select the BAKE function and preheat MAXX to 355ºF (179ºC).
2. In a bowl, combine the sugar, butter, egg, flour, and baking soda with a whisk. Stir in the bananas and walnuts.
3. Transfer the mixture to a greased baking dish. Put the dish in the air fryer oven and bake for 10 minutes.
4. Reduce the temperature to 330ºF (166ºC) and bake for another 15 minutes. Serve hot.

Chapter 10

Holiday Specials

Lush Snack Mix

Prep time: 10 minutes | Cook time: 10 minutes | Serves 10

- ½ cup honey
- 3 tablespoons butter, melted
- 1 teaspoon salt
- 2 cups sesame sticks
- 2 cup pumpkin seeds
- 2 cups granola
- 1 cup cashews
- 2 cups crispy corn puff cereal
- 2 cup mini pretzel crisps

1. In a bowl, combine the honey, butter, and salt.
2. In another bowl, mix the sesame sticks, pumpkin seeds, granola, cashews, corn puff cereal, and pretzel crisps.
3. Combine the contents of the two bowls.
4. Put the mixture in the air fryer basket. Select the AIR FRY function and cook at 370ºF (188ºC) for 10 to 12 minutes, shaking the basket frequently. Do this in two batches.
5. Put the snack mix on a cookie sheet and allow it to cool fully.
6. Serve immediately.

Hasselback Potatoes

Prep time: 5 minutes | Cook time: 50 minutes | Serves 4

- 4 russet potatoes, peeled
- Salt and freshly ground black pepper, to taste
- ¼ cup grated Parmesan cheese
- Cooking spray

1. Spray the air fryer basket lightly with cooking spray.
2. Make thin parallel cuts into each potato, ⅛-inch to ¼-inch apart, stopping at about ½ of the way through. The potato needs to stay intact along the bottom.
3. Spray the potatoes with cooking spray and use the hands or a silicone brush to completely coat the potatoes lightly in oil.
4. Put the potatoes, sliced side up, in the air fryer basket in a single layer. Leave a little room between each potato. Sprinkle the potatoes lightly with salt and black pepper.
5. Select the AIR FRY function and cook at 400ºF (204ºC) for 20 minutes. Reposition the potatoes and spritz lightly with cooking spray again. Air fry until the potatoes are fork-tender and crispy and browned, another 20 to 30 minutes.
6. Sprinkle the potatoes with Parmesan cheese and serve.

Air Fried Spicy Olives

Prep time: 10 minutes | Cook time: 5 minutes | Serves 4

- 12 ounces (340 g) pitted black extra-large olives
- ¼ cup all-purpose flour
- 1 cup panko bread crumbs
- 2 teaspoons dried thyme
- 1 teaspoon red pepper flakes
- 1 teaspoon smoked paprika
- 1 egg beaten with 1 tablespoon water
- Vegetable oil for spraying

1. Drain the olives and place them on a paper towel–lined plate to dry.
2. Put the flour on a plate. Combine the panko, thyme, red pepper flakes, and paprika on a separate plate. Dip an olive in the flour, shaking off any excess, then coat with egg mixture. Dredge the olive in the panko mixture, pressing to make the crumbs adhere, and place the breaded olive on a platter. Repeat with the remaining olives.
3. Spray the olives with oil and place them in a single layer in the air fryer basket. Work in batches if necessary so as not to overcrowd the basket. Select the AIR FRY function and cook at 400ºF (204ºC) for 5 minutes until the breading is browned and crispy. Serve warm

Holiday Spicy Beef Roast

Prep time: 10 minutes | Cook time: 45 minutes | Serves 8

- 2 pounds (907 g) roast beef, at room temperature
- 2 tablespoons extra-virgin olive oil
- 1 teaspoon sea salt flakes
- 1 teaspoon black pepper,
- preferably freshly ground
- 1 teaspoon smoked paprika
- A few dashes of liquid smoke
- 2 jalapeño peppers, thinly sliced

1. Select the ROAST function and preheat MAXX to 330ºF (166ºC).
2. Pat the roast dry using kitchen towels. Rub with extra-virgin olive oil and all seasonings along with liquid smoke.
3. Roast for 30 minutes in the preheated air fryer oven. Turn the roast over and roast for additional 15 minutes.
4. Check for doneness using a meat thermometer and serve sprinkled with sliced jalapeños. Bon appétit!

Hearty Honey Yeast Rolls

Prep time: 10 minutes | Cook time: 20 minutes | Makes 8 rolls

- ¼ cup whole milk, heated to 115ºF (46ºC) in the microwave
- ½ teaspoon active dry yeast
- 1 tablespoon honey
- ⅔ cup all-purpose flour, plus more for dusting
- ½ teaspoon kosher salt
- 2 tablespoons unsalted butter, at room temperature, plus more for greasing
- Flaky sea salt, to taste

1. In a large bowl, whisk together the milk, yeast, and honey and let stand until foamy, about 10 minutes.
2. Stir in the flour and salt until just combined. Stir in the butter until absorbed. Scrape the dough onto a lightly floured work surface and knead until smooth, about 6 minutes. Transfer the dough to a lightly greased bowl, cover loosely with a sheet of plastic wrap or a kitchen towel, and let sit until nearly doubled in size, about 1 hour.
3. Uncover the dough, lightly press it down to expel the bubbles, then portion it into 8 equal pieces. Prep the work surface by wiping it clean with a damp paper towel (if there is flour on the work surface, it will prevent the dough from sticking lightly to the surface, which helps it form a ball). Roll each piece into a ball by cupping the palm of the hand around the dough against the work surface and moving the heel of the hand in a circular motion while using the thumb to contain the dough and tighten it into a perfectly round ball. Once all the balls are formed, nestle them side by side in the air fryer basket.
4. Cover the rolls loosely with a kitchen towel or a sheet of plastic wrap and let sit until lightly risen and puffed, 20 to 30 minutes.
5. Uncover the rolls and gently brush with more butter, being careful not to press the rolls too hard. Place the rolls in the air fryer basket.
6. Select the AIR FRY function and cook at 270ºF (132ºC) for 12 minutes, or until the rolls are light golden brown and fluffy.
7. Remove the rolls from the air fryer oven and brush liberally with more butter, if you like, and sprinkle each roll with a pinch of sea salt. Serve warm.

Chapter
11

Fast and Easy Everyday Favorites

Bacon-Wrapped Jalapeño Poppers

Prep time: 5 minutes | Cook time: 12 minutes | Serves 6

- 6 large jalapeños
- 4 ounces (113 g) ⅓-less-fat cream cheese
- ¼ cup shredded reduced-fat sharp Cheddar cheese
- 2 scallions, green tops only, sliced
- 6 slices center-cut bacon, halved

1. Select the BAKE function and preheat MAXX to 325ºF (163ºC).
2. Wearing rubber gloves, halve the jalapeños lengthwise to make 12 pieces. Scoop out the seeds and membranes and discard.
3. In a medium bowl, combine the cream cheese, Cheddar, and scallions. Using a small spoon or spatula, fill the jalapeños with the cream cheese filling. Wrap a bacon strip around each pepper and secure with a toothpick.
4. Working in batches, place the stuffed peppers in a single layer in the air fryer basket. Bake for about 12 minutes, until the peppers are tender, the bacon is browned and crisp, and the cheese is melted.
5. Serve warm.

Indian-Style Sweet Potato Fries

Prep time: 5 minutes | Cook time: 8 minutes | Makes 20 fries

Seasoning Mixture:
- ¾ teaspoon ground coriander
- ½ teaspoon garam masala
- ½ teaspoon garlic powder
- ½ teaspoon ground cumin
- ¼ teaspoon ground cayenne pepper

Fries:
- 2 large sweet potatoes, peeled
- 2 teaspoons olive oil

1. In a small bowl, combine the coriander, garam masala, garlic powder, cumin, and cayenne pepper.
2. Slice the sweet potatoes into ¼-inch-thick fries.
3. In a large bowl, toss the sliced sweet potatoes with the olive oil and the seasoning mixture.
4. Transfer the seasoned sweet potatoes to the air fryer basket. Select the AIR FRY function and cook at 400ºF (204ºC) for 8 minutes, or until crispy.
5. Serve warm.

Purple Potato Chips with Rosemary

Prep time: 10 minutes | Cook time: 9 to 14 minutes | Serves 6

- 1 cup Greek yogurt
- 2 chipotle chiles, minced
- 2 tablespoons adobo sauce
- 1 teaspoon paprika
- 1 tablespoon lemon juice
- 10 purple fingerling potatoes

- 1 teaspoon olive oil
- 2 teaspoons minced fresh rosemary leaves
- ⅛ teaspoon cayenne pepper
- ¼ teaspoon coarse sea salt

1. In a medium bowl, combine the yogurt, minced chiles, adobo sauce, paprika, and lemon juice. Mix well and refrigerate.
2. Wash the potatoes and dry them with paper towels. Slice the potatoes lengthwise, as thinly as possible. You can use a mandoline, a vegetable peeler, or a very sharp knife.
3. Combine the potato slices in a medium bowl and drizzle with the olive oil; toss to coat. Transfer the potato slices to the air fryer basket.
4. Select the AIR FRY function and cook at 400ºF (204ºC) for 9 to 14 minutes. Use tongs to gently rearrange the chips halfway during cooking time.
5. Sprinkle the chips with the rosemary, cayenne pepper, and sea salt. Serve with the chipotle sauce for dipping.

Baked Cheese Sandwich

Prep time: 5 minutes | Cook time: 8 minutes | Serves 2

- 2 tablespoons mayonnaise
- 4 thick slices sourdough bread

- 4 thick slices Brie cheese
- 8 slices hot capicola

1. Select the BAKE function and preheat MAXX to 350ºF (177ºC).
2. Spread the mayonnaise on one side of each slice of bread. Place 2 slices of bread in the air fryer basket, mayonnaise-side down.
3. Place the slices of Brie and capicola on the bread and cover with the remaining two slices of bread, mayonnaise-side up.
4. Bake for 8 minutes, or until the cheese has melted.
5. Serve immediately.

Herb-Roasted Veggies

Prep time: 10 minutes | Cook time: 14 to 18 minutes | Serves 4

- 1 red bell pepper, sliced
- 1 (8-ounce / 227-g) package sliced mushrooms
- 1 cup green beans, cut into 2-inch pieces
- ⅓ cup diced red onion
- 3 garlic cloves, sliced
- 1 teaspoon olive oil
- ½ teaspoon dried basil
- ½ teaspoon dried tarragon

1. Select the ROAST function and preheat MAXX to 350ºF (177ºC).
2. In a medium bowl, mix the red bell pepper, mushrooms, green beans, red onion, and garlic. Drizzle with the olive oil. Toss to coat.
3. Add the herbs and toss again.
4. Place the vegetables in the air fryer basket. Roast for 14 to 18 minutes, or until tender. Serve immediately.

Classic Mexican Street Corn

Prep time: 5 minutes | Cook time: 7 minutes | Serves 4

- 4 medium ears corn, husked
- Cooking spray
- 2 tablespoons mayonnaise
- 1 tablespoon fresh lime juice
- ½ teaspoon ancho chile powder
- ¼ teaspoon kosher salt
- 2 ounces (57 g) crumbled Cotija or feta cheese
- 2 tablespoons chopped fresh cilantro

1. Spritz the corn with cooking spray. Working in batches, arrange the ears of corn in the air fryer basket in a single layer.
2. Select the AIR FRY function and cook at 375ºF (191ºC) for 7 minutes, flipping halfway, until the kernels are tender when pierced with a paring knife. When cool enough to handle, cut the corn kernels off the cob.
3. In a large bowl, mix together mayonnaise, lime juice, ancho powder, and salt. Add the corn kernels and mix to combine. Transfer to a serving dish and top with the Cotija and cilantro.
4. Serve immediately.

Peppery Brown Rice Fritters

Prep time: 10 minutes | Cook time: 8 to 10 minutes | Serves 4

- 1 (10-ounce / 284-g) bag frozen cooked brown rice, thawed
- 1 egg
- 3 tablespoons brown rice flour
- 1/3 cup finely grated carrots
- 1/3 cup minced red bell pepper
- 2 tablespoons minced fresh basil
- 3 tablespoons grated Parmesan cheese
- 2 teaspoons olive oil

1. In a small bowl, combine the thawed rice, egg, and flour and mix to blend.
2. Stir in the carrots, bell pepper, basil, and Parmesan cheese.
3. Form the mixture into 8 fritters and drizzle with the olive oil.
4. Put the fritters carefully into the air fryer basket.
5. Select the AIR FRY function and cook at 380ºF (193ºC) for 8 to 10 minutes, or until the fritters are golden brown and cooked through.
6. Serve immediately.

Corn Fritters

Prep time: 15 minutes | Cook time: 8 minutes | Serves 6

- 1 cup self-rising flour
- 1 tablespoon sugar
- 1 teaspoon salt
- 1 large egg, lightly beaten
- ¼ cup buttermilk
- ¾ cup corn kernels
- ¼ cup minced onion
- Cooking spray

1. Select the BAKE function and preheat MAXX to 350ºF (177ºC). Line the air fryer basket with parchment paper.
2. In a medium bowl, whisk the flour, sugar, and salt until blended. Stir in the egg and buttermilk. Add the corn and minced onion. Mix well. Shape the corn fritter batter into 12 balls.
3. Place the fritters on the parchment and spritz with oil. Bake for 4 minutes. Flip the fritters, spritz them with oil, and bake for 4 minutes more until firm and lightly browned.
4. Serve immediately.

Chapter 12

Sauces, Dips, and Dressings

Lemony Tahini

Prep time: 5 minutes | Cook time: 0 minutes | Serves 4

- ¾ cup water
- ½ cup tahini
- 3 garlic cloves, minced
- Juice of 3 lemons
- ½ teaspoon pink Himalayan salt

1. In a bowl, whisk together all the ingredients until mixed well.

Dijon and Balsamic Vinaigrette

Prep time: 5 minutes | Cook time: 0 minutes | Makes 12 tablespoons

- 6 tablespoons water
- 4 tablespoons Dijon mustard
- 4 tablespoons balsamic vinegar
- 1 teaspoon maple syrup
- ½ teaspoon pink Himalayan salt
- ¼ teaspoon freshly ground black pepper

1. In a bowl, whisk together all the ingredients.

Red Buffalo Sauce

Prep time: 5 minutes | Cook time: 20 minutes | Makes 2 cups

- ¼ cup olive oil
- 4 garlic cloves, roughly chopped
- 1 (5-ounce / 142-g) small red onion, roughly chopped
- 6 red chiles, roughly chopped (about 2 ounces / 56 g in total)
- 1 cup water
- ½ cup apple cider vinegar
- ½ teaspoon salt
- ½ teaspoon freshly ground black pepper

1. In a large nonstick sauté pan, heat ¼ cup olive oil over medium-high heat. Once it's hot, add the garlic, onion, and chiles. Cook for 5 minutes, stirring occasionally, until onions are golden brown.
2. Add the water and bring to a boil. Cook for about 10 minutes or until the water has nearly evaporated.
3. Transfer the cooked onion and chile mixture to a food processor or blender and blend briefly to combine. Add the apple cider vinegar, salt, and pepper. Blend again for 30 seconds.
4. Using a mesh sieve, strain the sauce into a bowl. Use a spoon or spatula to scrape and press all the liquid from the pulp.

Mushroom Apple Gravy

Prep time: 5 minutes | Cook time: 10 minutes | Serves 4

- 2 cups vegetable broth
- ½ cup finely chopped mushrooms
- 2 tablespoons whole wheat flour
- 1 tablespoon unsweetened applesauce
- 1 teaspoon onion powder
- ½ teaspoon dried thyme
- ¼ teaspoon dried rosemary
- ⅛ teaspoon pink Himalayan salt
- Freshly ground black pepper, to taste

1. In a nonstick saucepan over medium-high heat, combine all the ingredients and mix well. Bring to a boil, stirring frequently, reduce the heat to low, and simmer, stirring constantly, until it thickens.

Cauliflower Alfredo Sauce

Prep time: 2 minutes | Cook time: 0 minutes | Makes 4 cups

- 2 tablespoons olive oil
- 6 garlic cloves, minced
- 3 cups unsweetened almond milk
- 1 (1-pound / 454-g) head cauliflower, cut into florets
- 1 teaspoon salt
- ¼ teaspoon freshly ground black pepper
- Juice of 1 lemon
- 4 tablespoons nutritional yeast

1. In a medium saucepan, heat the olive oil over medium-high heat. Add the garlic and sauté for 1 minute or until fragrant. Add the almond milk, stir, and bring to a boil.
2. Gently add the cauliflower. Stir in the salt and pepper and return to a boil. Continue cooking over medium-high heat for 5 minutes or until the cauliflower is soft. Stir frequently and reduce heat if needed to prevent the liquid from boiling over.
3. Carefully transfer the cauliflower and cooking liquid to a food processor, using a slotted spoon to scoop out the larger pieces of cauliflower before pouring in the liquid. Add the lemon and nutritional yeast and blend for 1 to 2 minutes until smooth.
4. Serve immediately.

Chapter 13

Casseroles, Frittatas, and Quiches

Spinach Casserole

Prep time: 10 minutes | Cook time: 20 minutes | Serves 4

- 1 (13.5-ounce / 383-g) can spinach, drained and squeezed
- 1 cup cottage cheese
- 2 large eggs, beaten
- ¼ cup crumbled feta cheese
- 2 tablespoons all-purpose flour
- 2 tablespoons butter, melted
- 1 clove garlic, minced, or more to taste
- 1 ½ teaspoons onion powder
- ⅛ teaspoon ground nutmeg
- Cooking spray

1. Grease an 8-inch pie pan with cooking spray and set aside.
2. Combine spinach, cottage cheese, eggs, feta cheese, flour, butter, garlic, onion powder, and nutmeg in a bowl. Stir until all ingredients are well incorporated. Pour into the prepared pie pan.
3. Select the AIR FRY function and cook at 375°F (191°C) for 18 to 20 minutes, or until the center is set.
4. Serve warm.

Ritzy Vegetable Frittata

Prep time: 15 minutes | Cook time: 21 minutes | Serves 2

- 4 eggs
- ¼ cup milk
- Sea salt and ground black pepper, to taste
- 1 zucchini, sliced
- ½ bunch asparagus, sliced
- ½ cup mushrooms, sliced
- ½ cup spinach, shredded
- ½ cup red onion, sliced
- ½ tablespoon olive oil
- 5 tablespoons feta cheese, crumbled
- 4 tablespoons Cheddar cheese, grated
- ¼ bunch chives, minced

1. In a bowl, mix the eggs, milk, salt and pepper.
2. Over a medium heat, sauté the vegetables for 6 minutes with the olive oil in a nonstick pan.
3. Put some parchment paper in the base of a baking tin. Pour in the vegetables, followed by the egg mixture. Top with the feta and grated Cheddar.
4. Select the BAKE function and preheat MAXX to 320°F (160°C).
5. Transfer the baking tin to the air fryer oven and bake for 15 minutes. Remove the frittata from the air fryer oven and leave to cool for 5 minutes.
6. Top with the minced chives and serve.

Western Prosciutto Casserole

Prep time: 5 minutes | Cook time: 10 minutes | Serves 2

- 1 cup day-old whole grain bread, cubed
- 3 large eggs, beaten
- 2 tablespoons water
- ⅛ teaspoon kosher salt
- 1 ounce (28 g) prosciutto, roughly chopped
- 1 ounce (28 g) Pepper Jack cheese, roughly chopped
- 1 tablespoon chopped fresh chives
- Nonstick cooking spray

1. Select the BAKE function and preheat MAXX to 360ºF (182ºC).
2. Spray a baking pan with nonstick cooking spray, then place the bread cubes in the pan. Transfer the baking pan to the air fryer oven.
3. In a medium bowl, stir together the beaten eggs and water, then stir in the kosher salt, prosciutto, cheese, and chives.
4. Pour the egg mixture over the bread cubes and bake for 10 minutes, or until the eggs are set and the top is golden brown.
5. Serve warm.

Shrimp Green Casserole

Prep time: 15 minutes | Cook time: 22 minutes | Serves 4

- 1 pound (454 g) shrimp, cleaned and deveined
- 2 cups cauliflower, cut into florets
- 2 green bell pepper, sliced
- 1 shallot, sliced
- 2 tablespoons sesame oil
- 1 cup tomato paste
- Cooking spray

1. Select the BAKE function and preheat MAXX to 360ºF (182ºC). Spritz a baking pan with cooking spray.
2. Arrange the shrimp and vegetables in the baking pan. Then, drizzle the sesame oil over the vegetables. Pour the tomato paste over the vegetables.
3. Bake for 10 minutes in the preheated air fryer oven. Stir with a large spoon and bake for a further 12 minutes.
4. Serve warm.

Mini Quiche Cups

Prep time: 15 minutes | Cook time: 16 minutes | Makes 10 quiche cups

- 4 ounces (113 g) ground pork sausage
- 3 eggs
- ¾ cup milk
- Cooking spray
- 4 ounces (113 g) sharp Cheddar cheese, grated

Special Equipment:
- 20 foil muffin cups

1. Spritz the air fryer basket with cooking spray.
2. Divide sausage into 3 portions and shape each into a thin patty.
3. Put patties in air fryer basket. Select the AIR FRY function and cook at 390ºF (199ºC) for 6 minutes.
4. While sausage is cooking, prepare the egg mixture. Combine the eggs and milk in a large bowl and whisk until well blended. Set aside.
5. When sausage has cooked fully, remove patties from the basket, drain well, and use a fork to crumble the meat into small pieces.
6. Double the foil cups into 10 sets. Remove paper liners from the top muffin cups and spray the foil cups lightly with cooking spray.
7. Divide crumbled sausage among the 10 muffin cup sets.
8. Top each with grated cheese, divided evenly among the cups.
9. Put 5 cups in air fryer basket.
10. Pour egg mixture into each cup, filling until each cup is at least ⅔ full.
11. Switch from AIR FRY to BAKE. Bake for 8 minutes and test for doneness. A knife inserted into the center shouldn't have any raw egg on it when removed.
12. Repeat with the remaining quiches.
13. Serve warm.

Appendix 1 Measurement Conversion Chart

VOLUME EQUIVALENTS(DRY)

US STANDARD	METRIC (APPROXIMATE)
1/8 teaspoon	0.5 mL
1/4 teaspoon	1 mL
1/2 teaspoon	2 mL
3/4 teaspoon	4 mL
1 teaspoon	5 mL
1 tablespoon	15 mL
1/4 cup	59 mL
1/2 cup	118 mL
3/4 cup	177 mL
1 cup	235 mL
2 cups	475 mL
3 cups	700 mL
4 cups	1 L

VOLUME EQUIVALENTS(LIQUID)

US STANDARD	US STANDARD (OUNCES)	METRIC (APPROXIMATE)
2 tablespoons	1 fl.oz.	30 mL
1/4 cup	2 fl.oz.	60 mL
1/2 cup	4 fl.oz.	120 mL
1 cup	8 fl.oz.	240 mL
1 1/2 cup	12 fl.oz.	355 mL
2 cups or 1 pint	16 fl.oz.	475 mL
4 cups or 1 quart	32 fl.oz.	1 L
1 gallon	128 fl.oz.	4 L

TEMPERATURES EQUIVALENTS

FAHRENHEIT(F)	CELSIUS(C) (APPROXIMATE)
225 °F	107 °C
250 °F	120 °C
275 °F	135 °C
300 °F	150 °C
325 °F	160 °C
350 °F	180 °C
375 °F	190 °C
400 °F	205 °C
425 °F	220 °C
450 °F	235 °C
475 °F	245 °C
500 °F	260 °C

WEIGHT EQUIVALENTS

US STANDARD	METRIC (APPROXIMATE)
1 ounce	28 g
2 ounces	57 g
5 ounces	142 g
10 ounces	284 g
15 ounces	425 g
16 ounces (1 pound)	455 g
1.5 pounds	680 g
2 pounds	907 g

Appendix 2: Air Fryer Cooking Chart

Beef

Item	Temp (°F)	Time (mins)	Item	Temp (°F)	Time (mins)
Beef Eye Round Roast (4 lbs.)	400 °F	45 to 55	Meatballs (1-inch)	370 °F	7
Burger Patty (4 oz.)	370 °F	16 to 20	Meatballs (3-inch)	380 °F	10
Filet Mignon (8 oz.)	400 °F	18	Ribeye, bone-in (1-inch, 8 oz)	400 °F	10 to 15
Flank Steak (1.5 lbs.)	400 °F	12	Sirloin steaks (1-inch, 12 oz)	400 °F	9 to 14
Flank Steak (2 lbs.)	400 °F	20 to 28			

Chicken

Item	Temp (°F)	Time (mins)	Item	Temp (°F)	Time (mins)
Breasts, bone in (1 ¼ lb.)	370 °F	25	Legs, bone-in (1 ¾ lb.)	380 °F	30
Breasts, boneless (4 oz)	380 °F	12	Thighs, boneless (1 ½ lb.)	380 °F	18 to 20
Drumsticks (2 ½ lb.)	370 °F	20	Wings (2 lb.)	400 °F	12
Game Hen (halved 2 lb.)	390 °F	20	Whole Chicken	360 °F	75
Thighs, bone-in (2 lb.)	380 °F	22	Tenders	360 °F	8 to 10

Pork & Lamb

Item	Temp (°F)	Time (mins)	Item	Temp (°F)	Time (mins)
Bacon (regular)	400 °F	5 to 7	Pork Tenderloin	370 °F	15
Bacon (thick cut)	400 °F	6 to 10	Sausages	380 °F	15
Pork Loin (2 lb.)	360 °F	55	Lamb Loin Chops (1-inch thick)	400 °F	8 to 12
Pork Chops, bone in (1-inch, 6.5 oz)	400 °F	12	Rack of Lamb (1.5 – 2 lb.)	380 °F	22

Fish & Seafood

Item	Temp (°F)	Time (mins)	Item	Temp (°F)	Time (mins)
Calamari (8 oz)	400 °F	4	Tuna Steak	400 °F	7 to 10
Fish Fillet (1-inch, 8 oz)	400 °F	10	Scallops	400 °F	5 to 7
Salmon, fillet (6 oz)	380 °F	12	Shrimp	400 °F	5
Swordfish steak	400 °F	10			

Vegetables

INGREDIENT	AMOUNT	PREPARATION	OIL	TEMP	COOK TIME
Asparagus	2 bunches	Cut in half, trim stems	2 Tbsp	420°F	12-15 mins
Beets	1½ lbs	Peel, cut in ½-inch cubes	1Tbsp	390°F	28-30 mins
Bell peppers (for roasting)	4 peppers	Cut in quarters, remove seeds	1Tbsp	400°F	15-20 mins
Broccoli	1 large head	Cut in 1-2-inch florets	1Tbsp	400°F	15-20 mins
Brussels sprouts	1lb	Cut in half, remove stems	1Tbsp	425°F	15-20 mins
Carrots	1lb	Peel, cut in ¼-inch rounds	1 Tbsp	425°F	10-15 mins
Cauliflower	1 head	Cut in 1-2-inch florets	2 Tbsp	400°F	20-22 mins
Corn on the cob	7 ears	Whole ears, remove husks	1 Tbps	400°F	14-17 mins
Green beans	1 bag (12 oz)	Trim	1 Tbps	420°F	18-20 mins
Kale (for chips)	4 oz	Tear into pieces, remove stems	None	325°F	5-8 mins
Mushrooms	16 oz	Rinse, slice thinly	1 Tbps	390°F	25-30 mins
Potatoes, russet	1½ lbs	Cut in 1-inch wedges	1 Tbps	390°F	25-30 mins
Potatoes, russet	1lb	Hand-cut fries, soak 30 mins in cold water, then pat dry	½ -3 Tbps	400°F	25-28 mins
Potatoes, sweet	1lb	Hand-cut fries, soak 30 mins in cold water, then pat dry	1 Tbps	400°F	25-28 mins
Zucchini	1lb	Cut in eighths lengthwise, then cut in half	1 Tbps	400°F	15-20 mins

Appendix 3: Recipe Index

CPSIA information can be obtained
at www.ICGtesting.com
Printed in the USA
BVHW011050250421
605815BV00005B/416

9 781637 332061